hope rises from the land

hope rises from the land

by RALPH A. FELTON

FRIENDSHIP PRESS NEW YORK

All Bible quotations used in this book are from the Revised
Standard Version. Copyright, 1946 and 1952, by the Division
of Christian Education of the National Council of the Churches
of Christ in the United States of America.

missions - agricultural work

Library of Congress Catalog Card Number: 55–6841

contents

foreword

In the year 1820 William Carey, pioneer missionary to India, wrote, "In what ways can the comforts of distressed people be increased, their health better secured, and their general happiness promoted?" Even earlier, in 1794, he wrote home to his son, "Send me yearly the best garden and fruit seeds. Send also some implements of husbandry, scythes, sickles, and plough-wheels."

Missionaries since Carey have shown deep concern for the poverty of people on the land and have labored for improvement. They have laid some solid foundations and achieved notable results. However, they have too often worked barehanded and alone in an indifferent world that accepted poverty and hunger as facts of life that could not be changed.

But today village people everywhere have come to believe they need not remain impoverished forever, that something can and must be done. This rising hope among dispossessed people lays bare the need for expressing the gospel in practical and concrete ways.

It would seem that the words chosen by Christ to announce the purpose of his ministry were written especially for this hour!

> The Spirit of the Lord is upon me,
> because he has anointed me to preach good news to the poor.
> He has sent me to proclaim release to the captives
> and recovering of sight to the blind,
> to set at liberty those who are oppressed,
> to proclaim the acceptable year of the Lord.

Most mission boards today are increasing the number of missionaries consecrated and trained for practical forms of rural service. Sixteen centers for extension service in agriculture, health, and literacy have been opened during the past eighteen months. The work is usually done in cooperation with the village church and is related to projects of governments and private agencies.

Governmental programs of technical assistance, like those of missions, reflect a growing world conscience and concern for human need. Missionaries welcome these programs with their larger resources and are eager to cooperate in all appropriate ways. In some areas the fruits of these combined efforts may clearly be seen.

The people are moderate in their demands. They ask neither luxury nor political power, but some land to till, shelter, food, and clothing for their families. But their hope is rising, and peace will hardly come to the earth until these just needs are taken seriously. To make the best possible use of the resources God has provided constitutes the central challenge of our time.

This striving of dispossessed people for a better way of life is not new. It probably began two thousand years ago when Christ placed the hope of a more abundant life in the hands of his followers and then walked up the hill to Calvary. To lift the level of living in the midst of mass poverty is more than a technical or economic problem. It is also a moral and spiritual problem that summons the church to its greatest challenge and most noble opportunity since the days of William Carey.

The agricultural missionary becomes a trusted friend as he joins hands with the people and helps them work out solutions to the problems of food, clothing, and shelter in the spirit of Christ.

Dr. Felton has given his life to study, travel, and teaching in the field of The Rural Church and Christian Community Life, both at home and abroad. It is fitting that he should write this book on a type of Christian witness through which the church becomes a redeeming force that strives to save mankind not only from sin, but also from poverty and the other evils that blight both body and soul.

I. W. MOOMAW
Executive Secretary
Agricultural Missions, Inc.

New York 10, N. Y.
March 1, 1955

introduction

This book, *Hope Rises from the Land,* says to me, "Hope rises for the world." We in America find it hard to realize that all the rest of the world outside of western Europe is primarily and primitively agricultural. Dr. Felton has written so vividly and so simply and so close to the people that once having read these pages we should never again forget that this is so. He shows in bold silhouette, like a leafless tree on an icy winter morning, why Godless communism, ready to promise anything, has swiftly taken over so many areas of the world. To a man whose family is always starving and who has nothing material to lose, promises that later turn to mock him may seem rosy when they are made. Any condition, he reasons, will be better than that he is now in.

But Dr. Felton has offered us no mere antidote for communism. Rather, he has told us of a "contagious religion," that touches the whole of life, a positive, living Christianity in which there is no place for "isms."

Those of us in the farm field hope that these pages will be widely read by our missionary leaders. Some of us believe that the rural church in America can never adequately serve the people until its leaders make themselves more a part of the everyday life of the people and learn to speak their language; further, that its programs must be life centered. If we accept these premises for a highly-developed, highly-industrialized nation such as our own, how much more ought we to apply the principles in taking the gospel to some of the most primitive areas of the world.

In the green Garo Hills of Assam many had accepted the gospel, but they were starving to death. Then came an agricultural missionary to begin teaching them better farming as well. Now the people are calling their demonstration center "Garden Bari," the Garden of Eden. The missionary said, "I feel it is better to feed the hungry with steel plows than to fight them with steel bayonets."

1

High up in the Andes mountains in Ecuador, an Indian asked, "Can Christ help us to get our land back?" From the Foor Rural Life School in Angola, Africa, we get the report, "Our church . . . is growing 33 per cent a year and has more than ten thousand believers." A missionary in Japan chose to get out closer to the people and their everyday life. Better health, better schools, and better farming became a part of her daily work. Did evangelism suffer? Hear her answer: "I believe the church is growing faster with this type of program."

In a Lebanon village, the school work of a missionary center was based on an American curriculum. Its pupils used their training to get away from their rural environment, and the same old unsolved problems remained. Now at the Jibrail Rural Fellowship Center pupils are taught the things they can use at home. The once-poor village of Souboura has become prosperous.

Before the Kambini plan took hold in Mozambique, in southeastern Africa, many of the people had accepted Christian doctrine, but the old customs and beliefs hung on. The man of the family continued to believe that it was beneath him to go to the field and work. Let the women do that. The Kambini plan ties farm and home life with the gospel that is preached. Having seen its results firsthand, Dr. Felton concluded, "This type of agriculture is lifting people heavenward."

American farm people should find these stories particularly challenging. They will see many opportunities to give of their products, their know-how, and themselves, that Christ may be made known to all peoples and that peace and happiness may indeed come among men. Those who carry "with every sermon, a sample of garden seeds," even though it be a setting of eggs, a purebred bull, or a simple plow to replace an ancient hoe, should have the redoubled support of all of us who think of ourselves as farmers.

All professing American Christians should come to the last of these stories with a more real appreciation of the world responsibilities that are ours—and a greater determination to do more to meet them. From lands where "life doesn't begin at forty but ends at twenty-seven" and to which we send evangels for Christ, we may indeed get the message back, "You are all that we know about God."

ALEXANDER NUNN
Executive Editor
The Progressive Farmer

Birmingham, Ala.
March 1, 1955

a short trip to Mexico

A short trip to Mexico? Yes, indeed!
When your plane is some fifty miles southeast of Mexico City you land at the Tehuacán (Tay-wah-kan′) airport for a visit with Lester Zook.

Here in Tehuacán you leave the plane and shift to Zook's station wagon, which doubles as house and truck as the need arises. He's ready to start on an extension trip to the Oaxaca (Wah-hah′kah) area. The car is loaded with fertilizer, ant poison, rat poison, setting eggs, day-old chicks, vaccine, and a few small sacks of grain seeds.

Zook is a graduate of Pennsylvania State College and a former teacher of vocational agriculture at Waynesboro, Pennsylvania. He was sent to southeast Mexico by the Presbyterian Church, U. S. A., and is serving as a Christian county agent or missionary farmer.

At the first village, Tejupan (Tay-hoo′pan), you help Zook build compost piles. The Mexican soil has little humus in it. All of Mexico is poor compared with Zook's Pennsylvania Dutch community.

"When Mrs. Zook and I came here," he says, "we asked to be sent to one of the poorest and most backward areas. And we certainly were. The per capita income here is only one twentieth of what it is back in the States."

At the next stop, Telixtlahuaca (Tay-lees-tla-wa′ka), you help Zook lay off furrows for terracing the hillsides. As you were flying across Mexico you had noticed that nearly half the land was too mountainous or too dry to use. Someone on the plane had said that 46 per cent was like that, and the other 54 per cent appeared to be in need of irrigation.

Here at Telixtlahuaca, Zook shows you his demonstrations in strip cropping, contour plowing, and tree planting. The former Pennsylvanian and his Mexican colleagues are helping to bring soil conservation to this isolated corner of Mexico. Zook explains that he is not doing it alone.

3

Primitive plowing in southern Mexico. The Mexican Government and agricultural missionaries are rapidly inducing farmers to adopt more modern methods. Steel plows are replacing the kind shown in this picture.

By Burton Holmes, from Ewing Galloway, N. Y.

He cooperates with the farmers, the Mexican Government, and the Rockefeller Foundation.

While he is giving out some day-old chicks at the next stop, he tells you how he got started here with poultry.

"The Poultry Club and alumni of Penn State College helped me by sending the first purebred chicks. Next they sent me two incubators. I've certainly kept these incubators busy. I get requests for purebred chicks from all over the state of Oaxaca and seven other states as well.

"Some of these laying pullets are now producing 250 eggs a year. That's some better than the seventy record of the local hens."

"What does poultry raising have to do with missions?" someone asks.

"I feel like this," Zook explains: "I believe religion should improve all of life. My father back in Pennsylvania belonged to the Brethren-in-Christ Church. He taught us that way.

"Elizabeth, my wife, works a lot with the mothers on improving home life and health and all that. I think that's part of religion, too.

"You can see for yourself that these children need a better diet.

"Poultry increases the income of these people. Many of them give 10 per cent of their incomes to their churches. The lives of the poultry farmers are changed along with their flocks.

4

Lester Zook demonstrates the process of culling hens to young Mexican farmers.

"These seeds in the station wagon were developed here in Mexico by the Rockefeller Foundation. Here is a sack of sorghum for dry land. Here's some improved corn. Mexico's main crop is corn. That small bag has clover seed. It's great for building up the land. These are vegetable seeds. Elizabeth and I are trying to get some of these village people to eat something besides corn and beans for breakfast and beans and corn for supper.

"Before we'd been here a month we ran into the old familiar problem of drought. We persuaded a group of Evangelical Christians in the next community to dig a well for irrigation. It was some job to get the machinery working to take the water from the well to their fields, but when the crops were harvested the irrigated field produced three times as much as the dry fields.

"I want to introduce you to a man in the next village, Mr. Gildardo Santiago. He's a leader in the Presbyterian church there. He uses an irrigation well cooperatively with two of his neighbors. They've paid for the well and pump out of the profits from their increased crops in less than four years."

By the end of the day, you will have done about everything, from digging sanitary latrines in one village to culling hens in another.

At night, in the home of Gildardo Santiago, the movie projector and the portable generator get into action. Zook has films on better agriculture, health, and religion. That night for the first time you learn that both

5

A Mexican woman pats tortillas into shape with her hands. These corn-meal cakes and beans are the regular diet of rural Mexicans day in and day out.

Mr. and Mrs. Zook teach in the Presbyterian Bible School in Oaxaca. He teaches agriculture and rural evangelism. She teaches music and religious education.

It isn't too late after the meeting to start back to Tehuacán. There's less traffic at night. Besides, Les (his college name) is eager to make a trip to the "colony" tomorrow and invites you to go along, as it is something you might wish to see.

Next day you load up the station wagon again with corn and rice seed, in addition to eggs and ant poison and other things, and start east. You soon realize this is very different territory from yesterday's trip. A drop of about three thousand feet brings you to the lower coastal plain, and you shed your jacket.

6

As you ride along, Les explains that this colony is his first attempt to do what he has long felt to be the only real solution to the farm problem in the state of Oaxaca—move people from the mountainsides down into the lowland and put the mountains back into trees as they were meant to be. There will then be more room for those who remain.

"We thought that the mountain families might have trouble adapting to this hot climate," Les explains, "but one family from Nuxaa seemed to convince the others that the deep, rich, level soil more than makes up for what they suffer from the heat. The new drugs and D.D.T. help with the insect and malaria problems.

"Well, here we are," he says, as you turn off the road into what still seems to you like impenetrable jungle. You soon come to a couple of thatched huts and some patches of cleared land where corn and rice seem to be thriving among the tree stumps.

"Last year we had a good rice crop, but a number of families didn't get their land cleared and corn planted soon enough. In another year or so, when the government gets the new dam finished up the river, we hope to be able to plant around the calendar. It should furnish irrigation for a large area during the dry season, and later probably even electricity. We hope soon to have a road from Tehuacán directly to this area. The government is really interested in opening up these areas and increasing farm production. We are interested not only in better farm production but in a more abundant life for our Christian families, so that both people and churches can become self-supporting.

"Mexico is still a wide-open field for this type of work," Les explains. "The need is great. We are merely beginning to scratch the surface. There is very little extension work in Mexico. There is certainly need for hundreds of well-qualified young men like the fellows with whom I studied at Penn State College. They must be young men who have a vision of Christian service.

"I. W. Moomaw says a thousand more agricultural missionaries are needed to do this type of work. Wish we could have at least five of these thousand down here," he says, shifting to another chair, and then soberly, "Probably nothing would help more toward making the world a safer place in which to live and toward bringing about world peace."

But Lester Zook feels his is not an impossible task.

"It is a privilege," he says, "to help the other half or two thirds of the world who do not have our American know-how to get a start toward a better agricultural production and at the same time show them how they can work toward the conservation of the resources they have now."

7

This trip with Lester Zook, the evangelistic agriculturalist, will surely mean more to you than if you had gone to Mexico simply as a tourist with the 250,000 to 500,000 Americans who visit Mexico each year and watch bullfights, buy lottery tickets, and look down on the "natives."

an evening in a Mexican farm home

Will you attend a farmers' meeting in a Mexican home?

Mr. Claude Kellogg, an agricultural missionary, is to be the speaker, and his subject is "Corn."

The pastor of a new village church arranged the meeting. It is to be at the home of one of his members in a rural area near the village. This pastor is very proud of his new church, because his members built it without any aid from the outside.

As you reach the home where the meeting is to be held, you note that the house is the usual adobe. Adobe is warm in winter and cool in summer.

The main part of the house is separate from the kitchen. In practically all country homes here, the kitchen is across the patio from the rest of the house. The reason is that there is no chimney. Since the kitchen fire is built on the dirt floor between two or three stones, the kitchen soon fills with smoke. Therefore it's better to have it separate. Between this particular house and the kitchen is a patio about thirty feet wide. Here have been placed logs, boxes, wheelbarrows, carts, and a few chairs. Some fifty or sixty people, husbands and wives, are seated here waiting for the speaker.

By the feeble light of a lantern hanging from a rafter, Mr. Kellogg makes his drawings and explains the various methods of improving corn production. He explains how the basic need of Mexican soil is nitrogen, which can be had from plowing under green manures or cover crops.

Next he tells the farmers how they can increase their corn yield from 20 to 30 per cent by careful seed selection, germination testing, and disinfection.

Not a great increase, 20 per cent? It is much needed here, where corn is the staple diet.

Air, sunlight, and a sweep of attractive landscape are the greatest luxuries enjoyed by rural Mexicans who live in adobe huts like the one shown here.

The people sit for more than an hour listening and asking questions. You do not see their faces well because of the darkness, but enough to see how interested they are.

"We've heard about your church chickens," one man says. "Tell us, what is a church chicken?"

"They're just like any other chickens, except they're purebreds," the speaker explains.

"Generally a men's Sunday school class in some church north of the border sends me a hundred day-old chicks.

"The first thing I do is to inoculate them against Newcastle disease. Then I distribute them to the members of some church like this. The members raise them. When the chickens or the eggs are sold, a share is given to the church.

"Out of the last shipment of a hundred, we lost only one chick."

This meeting is typical of many held in rural Mexico. There is a patio shrouded in semidarkness, a feeble lantern light, a circle of intensely interested and hungry people.

As you walk back to the village with the Methodist missionary, you notice that he has a slight limp. It makes you wonder why he chose extension work, especially in a country like Mexico.

"Why did I choose extension?

"All around I saw fields producing below par. Animals were dying of diseases while their owners stood by helplessly. Insect pests were destroying crops while the people were living far below standard. In one village I saw a farmer, after four weeks of work day and night and after using all the money he could get, lose all his crop from a preventable disease. Poor fellow! Then I realized that our scientific knowledge is not just something to be taught in a classroom. It is a dynamic force. It should be dedicated to alleviate suffering like this fellow's and to increase production, raise the standard of living, and give hope and joy.

10   "In the Union Theological Seminary in Mexico City and in the Baptist Seminary in Tlalpan, I teach classes in poultry, horticulture, and beekeeping to the young Mexican pastors. The rest of my time I'm out working with Mexican farmers."

"What projects do you have besides corn and poultry?" someone asks.

"I give lots of time to fruit raising," he begins. "Have you been to Iztaccihuatl yet? It's a beautiful extinct volcano, usually covered with snow.

"At its foot is the village of San Felipe with a small church. About two hundred apple trees with large red and Golden Delicious apples now belong to the members of the church. When I made my first visit to San Felipe, I grafted some small branches from fine Missouri trees onto those

The faces of older Mexican farmers reflect the rigors of their long struggle to earn a livelihood from the soil. Younger farmers are eager to learn the new scientific methods that make crops less uncertain, life more secure. New pride comes when they realize their ability to provide needs and comforts for their families.

local trees or on the *tjocote,* a kind of haw or crab apple. You should see the apples now.

"You might say that this is the way I try to work. Graft something better onto what they now have.

"Beekeeping is also one of my main interests. The Mexican Government made me honorary technical adviser to the Department of Agriculture. I have written a forty-two-page bulletin on beekeeping that has been used all over Mexico. For five years I've had charge of the government apiary."

As you prepare to leave him in the humble home of the Mexican pastor, he tries to answer again that question as to how he happened to be an agricultural missionary.

11

"I was born in a Christian home in Wisconsin. I was headed toward missions by hearing a missionary from Africa talk about his work.

"I have never had one moment of regret that I'm an agricultural missionary. All over rural Mexico are people who know nothing of the simplest modern methods of agriculture. They're waiting for someone to lift them out of their poverty and superstition. When they get a chance they will listen spellbound, as they did in that farm home tonight. Many of them are taking up the new methods, trying them out, and getting the thrill of finding they really work wonders.

"Yes, I'm glad I'm an agricultural missionary."

the house of the friend

The dead mother was in a standing position, propped up by four men. A lifeless infant was on the bed.

Miss Cantrell says it was this unforgettable picture that led her to attempt work for Mexican motherhood.

"I had been led to the door of a home in the village of Los Haro," she continues. "The native midwife had disappeared, and the patient was dead. At her feet on the earthen floor was a lake of blood. She had emptied herself, they told me."

Miss Cantrell now has two maternity clinics, one here in Los Haro and another sixteen miles to the north in La Ermita, where she has a Mexican graduate nurse, Señorita Suarez, in charge.

The work has grown until a course has been added for training Mexican girls to become midwives. Six village girls are enrolled in this course. Three others have finished and now are serving in this big, needy territory.

12

Miss Cantrell and her Mexican associate ride horseback when they visit patients' homes in eighteen or twenty Mexican villages. Student nurses help with the care of expectant mothers who come to the maternity centers for delivery.

"Our working conditions are primitive," Miss Cantrell explains.

"Regardless of how clean we may be in handling a delivery, we know that if we leave our patient at 2 A.M., the father and sometimes as many as two of the children, in spite of our advice, will make their bed with the recently delivered woman and her newborn infant. If during the day they were cleaning the stable, it makes no difference. They neither remove nor change their clothing. It is all the same."

Miss Florine Cantrell is a registered nurse from Waynesboro, Tennessee, with additional training at the Maternity Center Association in New York City. She is working under the United Christian Missionary Society with headquarters at Indianapolis.

Her village of Los Haro has approximately one thousand people and is twelve miles out in the country in a large semidesert region called Jerez Valley, which is in the state of Zacatecas. This "valley" is more than a mile high. The only thing that is low about it is the standard of living of its people.

"On my train down through this Mexican plateau I noticed every little mud-hut village and wondered if I would have a chance to work in a place like that. How I wished that I might! I dedicated my life to the land and the people of this dry, barren, sun-scalded segment of the plateau."

Physicians are few in Mexico, approximately one third the number per thousand population as in the United States. Mexican doctors are mostly in the cities. The daily calories consumed by the average Mexican are only half what the average American gets. This adds up to a life expectancy in Mexico of thirty-seven years, slightly more than half as

13

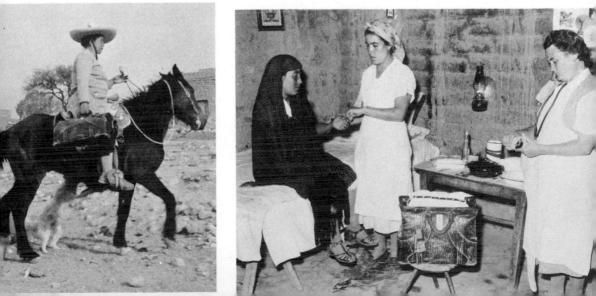

long as on this side of the Rio Grande. There are 120,000 rural communities in Mexico, and few of them have health facilities.

"We are driving with a sense of urgency," says Miss Cantrell, "in preparing local leadership in the various phases of our work.

"We are conducting prenatal clinics in from eighteen to twenty villages all the time."

Added to Miss Cantrell's health program, she and her colleagues have three churches, three Sunday schools, and five vacation church schools. She delivers babies, distributes medicines, gives lectures on sanitation, and teaches literacy classes.

When the mothers could not follow her instructions to add milk to the diet of undernourished children, because there was no milk to be had,

At far left, a Mexican smiles happily as he leads one of the French Alpine goats brought in by Miss Cantrell to add milk to the diet of undernourished children. A small girl shows her enthusiasm with even greater zest.

she brought in some French Alpine milch goats, which were crossed with the native goats.

"We have delivered babies for 706 women," explains Miss Cantrell, "with only one mother lost.

"One of our mothers said to me not long ago, 'Before you came to us, many graves were opened to receive mothers. Now all that has been changed.'"

This is the work of a country girl from a humble Tennessee home who, at the age of fourteen, heard a call that, as it came nearer, was to the mud huts of Jerez Valley in Mexico. Over the door of her home in the village of Los Haro someone has written the words *"La Casa del Amiga,"* which means "The House of the Friend."

15

a beautiful view in the high Andes

Flying south, high over the Andes, you see in the distance a tiny green strip, an oasis on the seared and thirsty slopes of Ecuador. It is your destination, Bella Vista, which means "beautiful view."

As your plane lands, you look around you and back up at the tall mountain peaks, many of them white with snow. You wonder who is so fortunate as to live at Bella Vista.

You are about twelve miles north of Quito (Kee'to), the capital of Ecuador, and only a short distance off the Pan-American Highway, built to bring the two Americas closer together.

You recall that someone said Ecuador is somewhat larger than California and has approximately as many people as Tennessee.

Here's Rolland Flory to meet you. He is the agriculturalist on this 185-acre Bella Vista mission farm operated by the Church of the Brethren.

"Tell us, Mr. Flory, what's the main idea here at Bella Vista?"

"We call this a Christian rural center," he begins. "It was started by one of our great missionaries, J. Benton Rhoades.

16

"Some missions have a school, some a church, some a health clinic, and some a farm. We try to wrap all four in one package and call it a Christian rural center."

"Aren't all these South American nations free countries? Why not leave them alone?"

"Yes, they have their political freedom. But the indigenous Indians are not free, by any means. They comprise about 60 per cent of Ecuador's population. It is among these landless Indians that we are working."

"What do you mean by landless Indians? In North America if an Indian doesn't have anything else, he has land."

"Here in Ecuador," Mr. Flory explains, "the Indians have been pushed back off the good land up into the Andes. In most of Ecuador the Indian

is the laborer for the well-to-do absentee landlord; the owner lives in the city and has most of the modern gadgets. All he does is advance cash and food to his Indian workers. They must work off this debt before they can change employers. Thus their freedom is lost for life. On the death of a farm hand, his debt is passed on to his children."

"Can't the American Government do something to help?"

"Yes," Mr. Flory says, "the American Government is doing something about it by sending agriculturalists under the Point Four program. These men work mostly with the large Spanish landlords. We missionaries cooperate with the Point Four men, but we give our time to the Indians, who make up 60 per cent of the population. We try to work where the need is greatest."

"Just what is your job here with these Indians, Mr. Flory?"

"Well, let's start at the bottom," says Mr. Flory. "The tools of the average Indian farmer are a wooden plow, two large hoes, a shovel, a small hand sickle, a bolo knife for cutting shrubs, and a five-foot stick for making holes in which to plant corn.

"We're now getting them to use an eight-inch moldboard plow. In order to do this I must attach the moldboard to their old wooden plows.

"I've also made a simple cylinder for threshing their oats. Before they

had this, they beat out the grain on the ground with a long stick.

"The top soil here is sandy and washes away easily. If you'll come with me, I'll show you how we're demonstrating the various methods of soil conservation.

"We're using eucalyptus trees to hold the soil on this steeper slope. Between here and the school, we're terracing. Beyond our electric plant and the tool shed we're contouring and strip cropping."

"Why not use more commercial fertilizer? Can't you get it here in Ecuador?"

"You can buy it here, but the Andean Indians have a per capita income of only forty-four dollars a year. They can't afford to buy it, so we get them to use green manure. And we're also introducing better livestock."

"Do you mean you give them purebred livestock like these that we see in your pasture?"

"No, we charge them a small fee for the use of our purebred males.

"I've had very good luck introducing trench silos.

"I spend a lot of time in extension work,

At top, an Equadorian Indian in traditional costume. Below, a young farmer employed at one of the agricultural missions. In the picture at the right, a hut with grinding stone, where corn is crushed into meal.

distributing better seeds, budding and grafting fruit trees, and vaccinating their stock against disease."

"How do you tie up your school, church, health clinic, and farming in one package, as you said a while ago?"

"Our church is at the center of our whole program. Let's take our school as an example. I give each of the fifty-four students a school garden. Each of the older children has a home garden like your vocational agriculture boys in high school back in the States. During their last year in school the students have a livestock project.

"You see, the Indians' diet is composed mostly of corn, squash, and cabbage. This leaves a bad vitamin deficiency, especially among the children. And so we have the school gardens.

"At the school lunch we teach children to eat new vegetables.

"Our Parent-Teacher Association ties up this school agriculture with the homes of the people.

"Then, of course, we're always working on the big problem of land ownership. These Indians of the high Andes still nourish the hope of recovering the land that was taken from their ancestors at the time of the Spanish invasion.

"They say that a young missionary was once preaching to a congregation of Indians about what Christ could do for them. One man's hand went up, and he asked the speaker, 'Can Christ help us get our land back?' "

In the area where Flory works about 75 per cent of the Indians now own small plots of land. Here they're getting their land back.

As your plane climbs beautiful snow-covered Cayambe Mountain again, heading southward, tiny green Bella Vista fades into the distance. But you will not forget how it is helping the Indian enter upon his rightful inheritance as a child of God.

Irrigation ditches such as this one carry water to the parched land of the mountain slopes, magically changing it to rich soil for a mission farm.

land reform in Bolivia

A beggar sitting on a chair of gold."

This is the way the Bolivians describe their country. The amazing wealth of their land in natural resources is surpassed only by the amazing poverty of their people.

But there is hope. The present government has nationalized the great tin mines owned by the so-called tin barons, and there is on foot a program to divide the large farm lands among the Indians.

Land reform, the change from peonage to land ownership, was pioneered by the Canadian Baptist Mission at Guatajata (Gwah-tah-hah' tah). A visit to this mission farm of two hundred acres, situated 12,500 feet above sea level, on top of the world, will show you the type of land reform that all South America needs.

Willard Chandler is the missionary here who describes this interesting experiment.

"For centuries the Indians of Bolivia," he explains, "have lived in a state of semifeudalism on large farms. Back in 1920 our mission became the administrator of this two-hundred-acre farm. With it came thirty-five Indian families as serfs or peons.

"For fourteen years we were not very different from slaveowners. But then it became clear that we were trying to establish a Christian order with its freedom and progress while maintaining on our farm the old unchristian medieval feudal system.

"From 1935 to 1940 we made the change. For five years the peons were put on probation. Each one of the thirty-five families was given a section of the farm. It was explained to them that if in the next five years they showed that they could till this land, build a moderate-sized one-room house with doors and windows to specifications, and in general demonstrate that they had the ability to manage their own affairs, the

At right, a view of the mission farm overlooking beautiful Lake Titicaca. Below, the llamas are in strange contrast with a modern tractor manned by a Bolivian farmer. At bottom of page, another view of the farm at Guatajata, where peons were changed into land owners, and the land reform movement in Bolivia began.

land they now occupied would be theirs. All but one family accepted the offer."

"And what changes did land ownership make among these Indians?"

"In the first place, their hovels were changed to homes, with tile roofs, windows, wooden floors, ceilings, wallpaper, and bedsteads.

"Then the schools began to fill up. We had given these people a good school, but for years it remained scarcely half full. They knew what we didn't know, that serfs do not need schools. They were no different from the hundreds of thousands of other Indians throughout these mountains—a people bound to land that was not their own, crushed by poverty from which they had no escape, their bodies diseased and their minds dwarfed.

"Now we have in this district not one school, but eighteen, with twenty-six teachers and 704 pupils.

"Next the church began to fill up. Old serfs became deacons, and young Indians became lay preachers to new communities. Now we have seventeen preaching points, with six organized churches."

"And your work, what do you do, Mr. Chandler?"

"My farm experience and training in Canada has helped me in managing this farm. Also I am head of our Bible school, which has thirty-six students in training to become teacher-preachers. Usually I preach five times each Sunday. Then I must supervise our building program. We have three new or remodeled school buildings."

As Mr. Chandler talks to you he points out these various buildings on the highest mission farm in the world. You look across the almost barren plain, girded about on either side by even higher mountain peaks. You see many farm colonies and hamlets tucked away in the valleys. Three fourths of these communities are now being served by schools and churches and by the wayside clinic that goes out from the Christian rural center.

In checking up on your visit to Guatajata, you have a chance to get an appraisal from the man who is in charge of all the rural schools of Bolivia. He is Señor A. Perez.

"We consider this the most successful of all projects to rehabilitate the Indian," are his words.

Then another Bolivian, this time a senator, has this to say, "This type of work should be extended all over Bolivia."

The Vice-President of Bolivia in an interview said, "The people at Guatajata gave us the basic draft for our present land reform."

The Evangelical church is succeeding in South America because while it is preaching salvation through the cross of Jesus Christ, it is not forgetting the agricultural problems of its people. At Guatajata, the mission is collaborating with Point Four of the American Government as it touches the promotion of 4-H Clubs, consumers' cooperatives, field experiments with insecticides, grasses, and wheat.

In this visit to the shores of Lake Titicaca one can see that the commission given two thousand years ago is still valid—to proclaim release to the captives and sight to the blind. The church can succeed as it faces the peonage system, the number one social and economic problem of South America.

the Garden of Paradise

You're flying to Chile? Be sure to see the farm school at El Vergel.

This shoestring country is about the shape of a snake. It is only a hundred miles wide, but as long as from Boston to San Francisco.

Northern Chile looks like a desert. You are told that copper and nitrates are the main crops here. The nitrates are used for commercial fertilizer to improve farms or for munitions to kill off farmers' sons.

Central Chile seems to have only rich farm lands. One report states that 40 per cent of all Chileans live by agriculture. If working for small wages on large estates is "living," this is true.

On one estate, you are told, there are four thousand workers but not a single piece of modern machinery.

Your plane lands at the southern end of this rich, irrigated valley, where the red hills of the southland begin. This is El Vergel (pronounced El Ver-hail'). The name means "Garden of Paradise."

The agricultural missionary you meet here is Mr. Elbert Reed, trained at Iowa State College of Agriculture.

As you look around, you are surprised at the size of the place, and you ask Mr. Reed, "Is this a school or a ranch or an experiment station?"

"It's more than a school or a ranch or an experiment station. It's a training ground in Christian democracy for all of Chile," he explains.

"We have 3,800 acres. On this side of the Malleco River there are 750 acres of rich bottom irrigated lands. On ninety acres of this we raise nursery stock that is sent all over Chile. Our orchards cover two hundred acres. We send apples out by the shipload. We have a twenty-acre garden. We milk fifty cows and keep some two hundred hogs.

"Our main crop here is boys. We are training approximately sixty boys all the time in our three-year course. They are graduated, then go out and improve rural life throughout Chile.

"On those red hills across the river, there was once typical worn-out land. We're building it up by reforestation, cover crops, and permanent pasture."

"How is this different from any other good farm?" someone asks.

"Here at El Vergel we believe that *people* must develop along with *things*. We have 250 workmen here, a total of about nine hundred people with their families. They have a school, a church, health service, a consumers' cooperative, and various clubs. One of these workmen who was illiterate when he came has risen to the position of governor of a province."

"Who planned this whole program?"

"No one knows enough to do that," Reed explains. "We met each problem as it came along. When I came here in August, 1920, I found no apple trees had been sprayed for apple scab. It was late then for spraying, but I made some spray material of lime and sulphur, and with my poor Spanish, a workman's poor English, and a repaired spray machine, we got the apple scab under control. The spraying of fruit trees is now standard practice in all of Chile.

"When the apple tree was first brought to Chile the plant louse known as woolly aphis came along, but without the main controlling parasite,

the aphelinus mali. We flew some of these tiny insects in on an airplane over the Andes from Uruguay. We established them in our orchards, and they soon got the woolly aphis under control. Then we distributed colonies by the hundreds throughout Chile. The people didn't know what to think.

" 'Those Americans could have cleaned up thousands of pesos on that insect,' they said, 'but here they are, giving it away free!' "

"We knew that Chile was being served," Reed continues. "We wanted that to be a concrete example of applied Christian living.

"Shortly after I arrived here at El Vergel, I noticed the gullying of a field at the foot of one of those sharp, bare slopes that you see across the river. It was five years before we started planting trees there, but that beginning has mushroomed into approximately nine hundred acres of forest. The trees control soil erosion and provide timber.

"There was another problem. About two thirds of this farm is what we call red hill land. It is typical of millions of

25

Reading from top to bottom, the pictures show an artificial lake being stocked with fish, a first year student learning how to cultivate the soil, and the sawmill at El Vergel.

acres and thousands of farms in Chile. I took it as my major problem. I soon found we were operating it at a loss. Hundreds of thousands of people in Chile depend directly or indirectly on that type of land.

"I've spent twenty years studying that red hill land. As a result, a new type of agriculture has emerged. It is setting a pattern for all similar land in Chile. The land that once was devoted almost exclusively to wheat and oats now is covered with blue and white lupines, three kinds of grasses, and three or four clovers. With them have come silos, dairy cattle, ponds, fences, and profits.

"We publish bulletins on the results of our dry land farming, which we send to all parts of Chile. The government has asked me to serve on a national Soil Conservation Commission.

"All these things add up to their influence on people. Improved diet means improved people, who have a new outlook on life. The Christian viewpoint in life is emphasized constantly."

"Whatever led you to become an agricultural missionary, Mr. Reed?" you ask as you prepare to leave. "It seems to be such big and important work."

"Bishop Oldham of the Methodist Church wrote me that I was needed here," he explains. "I have always remembered the words he wrote on the margin of that letter. 'We want you. We need you. There is work that will fill your heart, your head, your hands.'

"It has."

the devil under a microscope

They come from many miles to see the devil. Even African pastors, deacons, and deaconesses come to the laboratory of Alice Strangway to see for themselves real *ovilulu* (evil spirits).

Many Africans believe that devils or evil spirits bring their diseases.

"This one is the bacillus of tuberculosis," explains Mrs. Strangway. "This disease abounds and is spreading rapidly, due to poor sanitation and faulty nutrition."

One pastor looks at it a long time. "If we had only known about it," he sighs.

Next they watch the moving microfilaria that causes so much blindness in Angola. How could there be a worse devil!

"Here are the red and blue stained parasites of malaria."

"Three of my six babies left us because of these," one mother sighs. She has the same deep sorrow that mothers have in every land.

What a collection of devils to be seen through one microscope! Rickets, pellagra, anemias, goiter, scurvy, diarrhea, and many more.

Africa's native religion is based upon devils. Witchcraft is a religion of evil spirits. The weird witch doctor in every village stays in business to cast out just such evil spirits.

27

Many leave this laboratory and return to their villages to spread the lessons they have learned. For them belief in witchcraft is gone forever. They learn how to cast out devils—by the food they eat.

Who is this lady who casts out devils?

When she was a high school student in Simcoe, Ontario, she decided she wanted to be a missionary. At the University of Toronto she heard about the need for missionary teachers of household science. She majored in that field. At a Student Christian Movement meeting she met a young medical student who was headed toward Africa.

For twenty-five years Dr. and Mrs. Walter E. Strangway, from the United Church of Canada, have been rendering a significant service to the sick and hungry people of Angola, Portuguese West Africa.

We are now at Chisamba Hospital in Angola. Alice Strangway is in her laboratory.

On the table beside her is a rack containing a dozen test tubes that are in use. Another large tray contains twenty or thirty bottles filled with reagents for testing chemical substances. A dish of pipettes is nearby. A monocular and a binocular microscope are also on the table.

"Tell us just a little about your job, Mrs. Strangway."

"Almost every African is hungry," she begins. "If he's not hungry from too little food, he's hungry from a badly balanced diet. The children suffer greatly. Babies at two or three years of age often do not weigh more than a one-year-old child who has been breast fed."

"What keeps the babies from growing as they should?"

"When weaning occurs, no suitable substitute for mother's milk is given them. This accounts for the many poorly-nourished children. Many children, adults too, have swollen bodies from the lack of good protein foods.

"Tuberculosis abounds. It's spreading rapidly, as it always does under

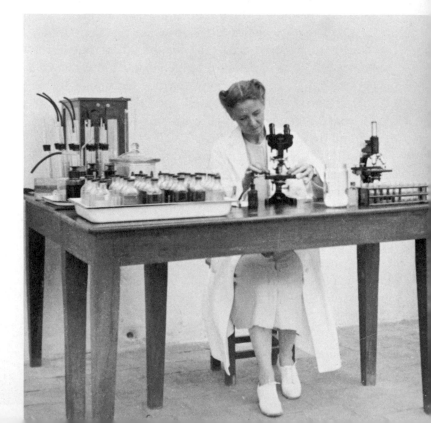

conditions of poor sanitation with poor nutrition. The African's diet is lacking in vitamins, minerals, and fats, as well as in good protein content."

"Isn't it very discouraging to work here?" you ask Mrs. Strangway.

"Just the opposite," she protests.

"When I first came out I supervised the teaching of household science in our girls' school. Then I thought I'd start what we call well-baby clinics. I soon had over four hundred babies and their mothers enrolled. We weighed each baby monthly and watched its growth. We found we could actually prevent many of these deadly African diseases. It was exciting to watch those babies grow instead of die."

"How did a Canadian like you come to know about African diseases?"

"At the University of Toronto I majored in food chemistry. I learned how to do research. One of my projects, I remember, was to study the effect of Vitamin B Complex on pigeons.

"When I came out here I worked closely with my husband in the hospital. I could not put out of my mind the army of sick people who came to the hospital with diseases I was sure could be prevented.

"With my husband's help I developed a well-equipped laboratory here in the hospital. From then on there was nothing so interesting as my work.

A laboratory assistant smiles as he looks at the "devils" under the microscope, confident that with modern medicine he can exorcise them.

29

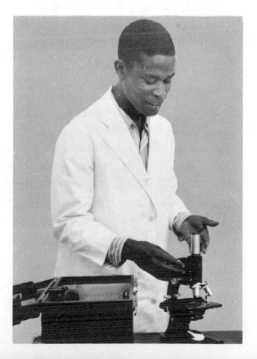

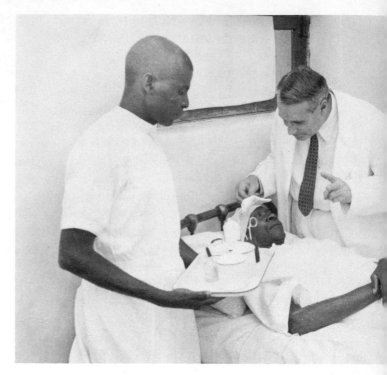

A thrilling moment comes to a patient who has undergone an operation for cataracts when Dr. Strangway removes the bandages and he realizes he can see again after having been blind.

"Back in Toronto for a year's furlough, I went to the Banting Institute of Medical Research. There I learned the technique of doing pathological sections. Later I studied tropical medicine in the University of Liverpool.

"On each of my three furloughs, instead of going around making speeches, I kept on working at my graduate research. I studied food technology, vitamin assay, dietetics, pathological chemistry, and public health nutrition.

"Then, of course, I tackle each problem here as it comes. In 1946, early in the school year, there were 166 of our 250 students with severe signs of malnutrition. Twenty-one had edema (swollen bodies). After six weeks of dietary treatment the trouble cleared up.

"Until 1940 there was no effective treatment available for the African disease called onyalai. The mortality rate usually reached about 90 per cent. In our laboratory here we found the cause of the disease. It was a deficiency of ascorbic acid.

"We administered filtered lemon juice intravenously with sterile saline solution to forty-three patients. Synthetic ascorbic acid was not available. All but one recovered in a few days."

"Why don't you pass on the results of your experiments to other missionaries, Mrs. Strangway?"

She turns to her desk and brings out reprints of her research from the American Medical Association, from the *Canadian Medical Association Journal,* from the Archives of Internal Medicine, and from the American Dietetic Association.

Her work is multiplied also as she trains African nurses, medical assistants, midwives, and leper injectors.

"Mrs. Strangway, what are you working on now?"

"Just now I'm studying the beneficial effects of feeding peanut meal, of which there is an abundance in Africa.

"I'm also spending more and more of my time in my laboratory training my African assistants.

"They have been taught since infancy to believe in witchcraft. They have been taught that devils or evil spirits bring disease. They see these devils now through the microscope. They are learning to cast out the evil spirits by eating properly balanced meals.

"In place of their belief in witchcraft, a great many of these people in Angola are learning to know the loving God who gives abundant life."

"How are you and your brilliant surgeon husband working together now, Mrs. Strangway?"

"While he's performing about seven hundred operations a year, I'm caring for the many cases of malnutrition that still come to the hospital.

"While he and his assistants cared for 1,432 bed patients last year and 11,200 outpatients, I was busy in the laboratory discovering a way to cure just one common African disease."

31

"Have you any message to send home with us, Mrs. Strangway?"

"Yes. Tell them Africa is hungry.

"Africa is hungry both for food and for the gospel.

"The church in Africa can never be strong while the majority of its membership continues to live below the minimum nutritional requirement for health.

"If you have any sons or daughters, tell them Africa needs more missionaries trained in agriculture and in nutrition.

"They will love to share with these underprivileged people some of their knowledge, as I have loved it. In this way they can do what they most want to do—build a better world."

new jobs for Ag students

New jobs are opening for agriculturally-trained young men.

Take Africa as an example. You could put continental United States down in it four times. It's a huge rural continent. One report states that 95 per cent of its 62,040 churches are rural.

A hundred years ago when our missionaries set out for Africa, they came from American farms. Four out of five Americans were rural in 1860. Even forty years ago our rural population in America was larger than the city group.

As these missionaries from American farms went back to Africa after each furlough they took with them improved seeds and fruit trees. A Mr. W. T. Currie in 1900 took improved poultry, pigs, sheep, and goats. Another missionary, William C. Bell, took plows with him when he opened his station in 1906. The Africans in that area own over a thousand plows now. William Sanders in 1912 introduced Carolina rice, which is now a staple product throughout his province. One missionary, William Cummack, in 1910 introduced soya, taro, and tea. Many more agricultural improvements came from those early missionaries.

Today two thirds of our people in America are city folk. When they go out as missionaries they have little knowledge of agriculture.

"We can see a change in our missionaries' interest in agriculture as America has changed from a rural to an urban society. Many of our missionaries today do not know about planting trees and seeds as they would if they had been brought up in rural America sixty years ago."

These are the words of Nathaniel Roe, a Cornell graduate in agriculture who arrived in Africa in 1951.

One of the first things Mr. Roe did after reaching his field, the French Cameroun in West Equatorial Africa, was to get in touch with each of the 105 members of his mission to see what their attitudes were regarding agriculture. He was eager that agricultural improvement should not be his program alone, but a part of the entire mission program. He wanted the educational and evangelistic missionaries to feel that his purpose or objectives were the same as theirs, also that they were cooperating with him in the special assignment he was carrying out in his work as an agricultural missionary.

Mr. Roe found that the early missionaries imported or brought fruit trees or new seeds with them. They seemed to have a real crusading interest in the agricultural needs of their people. It was the older missionaries who had planted the trees that he found at nearly every mission station.

He sent a questionnaire about agricultural missions to forty-four missionary families of the Presbyterian Church, U. S. A., in that section of Africa. Twenty-two of them replied.

Although this is a rural area, one third of these missionaries did not even have a garden.

One of the missionaries wrote, "From the ivory tower of one who knows nothing about agriculture, it seems wiser to use more effectively such means—tools, etc.—as the people already have, rather than disregarding them and introducing new things. That goes for animals and to a certain extent food, also."

This missionary could not have preferred the short-handled, back-breaking hoe or the sharp stick to the moldboard plow that puts the humus back into the soil and holds the moisture, if he had ever had any contact with agriculture in America.

This new type of missionary, going to serve a rural country like Africa with only an urban background, points clearly to the need for more specially-trained agricultural missionaries like Nathaniel Roe.

Nat Roe, as his friends affectionately call him, grew up on a dairy farm in Orange County, New York.

He majored in extension teaching at Cornell, taking subjects in every major field of agriculture, having as his adviser Professor Lincoln Kelsey, whose agricultural knowledge and interests are world-wide. Also at Cornell he met Muriel Osgood (Ozzie), a graduate in veterinary medicine, who has accompanied him on his African safari "for better or for worse."

Mr. Roe follows what he calls a three-point program. At first he studies conditions at the farm or village level. In doing this he has traveled the length and breadth of his mission area, visiting all but four of the mission stations. His second point is similar—experiment and research. His third phase is training African workers. He is now starting on the second and

Nathaniel Roe, inspecting the bean crop with a young African, seems pleased with the yield. The smiles of students in the garden indicate that they, too, are well satisfied with the harvest that modern scientific methods have helped them coax from the land.

third phases of his plan at Libamba, where he has 280 acres available for different types of agriculture.

He is teaching his students vegetable and fruit production, animal husbandry, disease control, sanitation, construction, agricultural engineering, and soil care. He and his wife together are equipped to handle such a curriculum.

In their leisure time during the past year, Nat and Ozzie have planted gardens, built a dormitory, started the distribution of purebred cockerels, and built a classroom as well as their own home. Clearing the land has its own complications, for it is covered with a dense growth of tangled vines and bushrope, binding all the branches into a dense barrier. The Roes expect to use about seven acres for their poultry project and about ten acres for swine.

Their training program is on two levels. On the apprentice level the students are trained to return to their homes to become village leaders. The other students are being trained to be teachers. All students are given Bible training. They are taught to teach and preach in their home villages. Mr. Roe feels that his missionary colleagues are cooperating well in this agricultural program. He is helping the Africans to a better knowledge of the love of God by showing them how to achieve a higher standard of living and a more abundant life.

It is young people like Nat and Ozzie Roe that Agricultural Missions, Inc., is helping to select and train for the fifty underdeveloped countries throughout the world. Out of fifteen thousand missionaries from the United States and Canada, only about a hundred have such training now. Over a thousand more are needed.

35

The school where Mr. Roe instructs future farmers is here shown in construction. Students contributed a large part of the labor needed to put up the building.

over a cup of coffee

Y ou who drank coffee or cocoa for breakfast this morning are invited to visit a fifteen-hundred-acre farm in Liberia where you can see these crops grow.

This farm is owned by the Protestant Episcopal Church. It is a part of Cuttington College and Divinity School.

You may need to refresh your memory as to where Liberia is. It is on the West Coast of Africa, is about the size of Ohio, and has about as many people as Iowa. You will feel at home here because English is the official language. Someone explains, however, that the country has eight major languages and as many as thirty-two dialects.

From Monrovia, the seaport town and capital, you travel 134 miles inland with a pickup truck until you come to a one-hundred-hut village called Swacocoa. This means "cocoa town." Here is a real college, where teachers, preachers, and farmers are trained.

The man you will want to see is Fenton Sands. He runs this fifteen-hundred-acre school farm, with which he hopes to make the school self-supporting. He also supervises a two-hundred-acre school farm at Bromley, where rubber and citrus fruits are produced. He has still another three-hundred-acre school farm at Bahlsmer, where he raises oil palms and yams.

It looks as though such a job would be too big for one man until you find that he has been trained especially for this task. He had four years in the Cornell College of Agriculture and later came back for his Doctor's degree in the Department of Pomology (the science of fruit growing).

"Our main money crops," he explains, "are coffee, cocoa, and oil palms. We have five hundred acres in coffee trees, three hundred acres in cocoa, and one hundred acres in oil palms. Also, we have twenty-five acres of citrus fruit, fifteen acres of ginger, and five acres of pineapple.

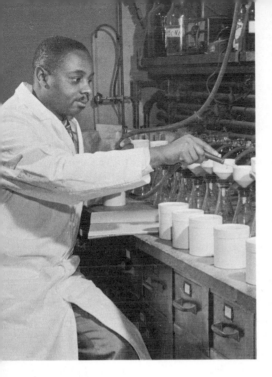

Fenton Sands learned the know-how of his present work through years of painstaking laboratory training. He serves in a Liberian village like the one shown below.

"We have moved our rice down from the hillsides to the swamp land. We are trying to teach everybody to plant trees instead of rice on the slopes in order to hold the soil.

"We have a garden big enough to raise the vegetables to feed our forty-five students. Usually we have some forty head of cattle, twenty-five hogs, and approximately five hundred laying hens."

"Who does all the work on this fifteen-hundred-acre ranch?" you ask.

"Ten students who work as apprentices for a two-year period," Mr. Sands tells you. Although he teaches two agricultural classes in the school, he finds this supervised farm work is the best way to train farmers.

"What is your farm plan, Mr. Sands, or what are you trying to accomplish?" you ask, because everything here seems very different from farming back home in America.

"Proper land utilization is my first concern," he tells you. "If you had been here for a few years, you would have seen the land getting poorer every year. I want to get tree crops on all the hillsides to hold the soil and improve the land.

"Then I want to show the people how to raise some cash crops. In this way they will learn that they can afford to have schools, churches, and a

37

Cocoa beans, seen here in the process of drying, help pay the expenses of Fenton Sands' mission.

higher standard of living. We ship our coffee, cocoa, and oil-palm products to you in America and let you help our missionary work when you purchase them."

"Well, now, I never thought of missionary work like that. A good idea you have there!"

"Dorothy, my wife, is a home economics teacher from Hunter College. She is trying to get the people to increase their protein intake. That's the reason we're producing our eggs, meat, poultry, and soya beans. She is conducting prenatal and postnatal clinics, while I'm draining swamps to starve mosquitoes and stop malaria."

"Mr. Sands, these tree crops are new to us in America. How long does it take them to get into production?" you ask.

"Cocoa trees get into production in five years, coffee trees in three years, ginger in fourteen months and bananas in twelve."

The Episcopal Board of Missions sent Mr. Sands to Costa Rica for five months to study coffee and cocoa production. For his Doctor's thesis he studied the relationship between the chemical analyses of the leaves and the chemical and physical analyses of the soil to find out how to feed the soil in order to grow better coffee and cocoa.

"What made you decide to come out here to Liberia as an agricultural missionary?" someone asks.

"I think it was my experience in the armed services," he explains. "I saw the needs of the people in other parts of the world. I felt I wanted to get into something more constructive than war."

Before leaving, you want to know one more thing. "Do you feel satisfied with the job you are doing here, Mr. Sands?"

He answers this way:

"I feel that we are making progress here at the school and on the farm. I am giving half my time to extension work. I have an area here of some twelve thousand square miles. I need a one-thousand-egg incubator to expand our poultry work. I am helping the Liberian farmers build up home poultry flocks from American breeds. I need another tractor, and I want to build a laboratory so I can teach the Liberian students how to make soil and leaf analyses and how to feed this worn-out soil. They are really good students, eager to learn."

As you leave, you remember having heard at a church missionary program about Bravid Harris, a minister from Virginia, elected a bishop of the Episcopal Church and sent to Liberia. You recall that he made a survey to find out the needs of his field. That was in 1945.

Today, on this land given to Bishop Harris by the Liberian Government for his schools, you have just met two of the missionaries he selected and trained, Fenton and Dorothy Sands, from New Jersey. You have seen the good results that their consecrated training has produced. And you have caught a glimpse of the possibilities of the future if such work continues to grow, by seeing how Mr. and Mrs. Sands are working together to change their little corner of Africa, called Liberia.

Below, a Liberian skillfully balances a bowlful of rice on her head. At right, a young workman beats the rice into supper meal.

conquerors of the jungle

Frank James went to Africa to hunt big game. While there, he was killed by a wounded elephant. His sister gave the money to start an industrial school there in Africa in his memory.

Hal Thwing, a graduate in engineering from the University of Washington, is running that school.

Both young men went out to conquer the jungle. Both were well prepared.

A visit to this Frank James Industrial School at Elat in the French Cameroun shows you how Mr. Thwing is helping to change African life.

A tall man, wearing glasses, with his hair combed straight back from a high forehead, comes toward you. It is Hal Thwing.

"We'll start over here where the logs come in," he begins. "This is Nkoo Abomo. He teaches the students how to run the sawmill."

Mr. Abomo appears to be about fifty. Although he takes pride in his job, he informs you that he is also an elder in the Elat church.

"Our church probably has the largest membership of any Presbyterian church in the world," he continues. You begin to feel that this is more than a school you are visiting. It is a great Christian community.

Next you meet Ayissi Yana, who is making armchairs.

"This man has made his own table saw. He turns out armchair parts on a big scale.

"Our students made three hundred new desks this year for our mission schools."

As you pass one machine after another, you see young Africans making all types of furniture. When you get away from the noise you ask Hal who will ever use all this modern furniture.

"The home of the primitive African is bare," he begins. "Our eighty students are changing that pattern.

"I see from our records that during the past year our students have made 27 dressing tables, 16 chests of drawers, 24 wardrobe cupboards, 12 tables, five food cupboards, three desks, and three bookcases for missionaries; plus 100 armchairs, 150 dining room chairs, 80 beds, and 20 tables for Africans.

"By using these machines, we emphasize mass production," Mr. Thwing continues. "That cuts selling prices and makes it possible for Africans to purchase the things they need. Our students make this furniture you see for half the cost that is quoted by the local European cabinet makers.

"As a result of these machines, the take-home pay has doubled, and the cost of furniture has been halved. Our students accomplish as much now in two weeks as they did previously in two months. Civilization is not geographical nor racial. It's how we *work* and *live*.

"I want you to meet this student. This is Zilli Moise. He's studying auto mechanics.

"As you have noticed out on the roads, the Africans carry their loads on their heads or on their backs. We're teaching our students how to use and repair automobiles and other machinery.

"One boy, after his four years here, runs a repair shop on a cotton plantation. Primitive customs must be changed in this way, one at a time.

"Here's a graduate, now running the forty horsepower diesel that provides the power for our school.

"The African who works with hand tools is not extinct, but I believe his days are numbered. We are teaching our boys how to use machinery. We are trying to teach our young Christians to help themselves and never be objects of charity.

41

"Africans have been living in mud huts. We're teaching our students how to make houses of bricks and cement blocks and install electrical equipment. They learn how to make doors and windows.

"The cottage that you see there, our students are just completing. It's for girl students. Our graduates are building houses like that all over the French Cameroun.

"Many of the buildings of our Presbyterian Mission in the French Cameroun have been constructed by our students.

"They attend classes about half time and work in the shops half time. Our school is 80 per cent self-supporting. The other 20 per cent is paid by our Presbyterian Mission.

Genial-faced Hal Thwing is proving that even jungles cannot resist faith, knowledge, and hard work.

"All our students must be graduates of their local or elementary schools before they come here. They must also be professing Christians, although not necessarily fully-trained church members. We screen our entering students carefully. We admitted only 69 out of 250 applicants for the last entering class.

"Each student learns to be a mason, carpenter, electrician, draftsman, and mechanic. This doesn't mean that every African student learns everything about all these trades.

"One of the main purposes of the school is to build men of Christian character. Our graduates are found among the leading laymen of many of the churches in the French Cameroun."

These are the methods that Hal Thwing and his colleagues are using to

Students at the Frank James Industrial School are taught such skills as auto mechanics and how to care for and run diesel engines.

bring civilization to Africa. Hal's father is an engineer and a Presbyterian elder in Seattle. At a youth conference, Hal dedicated his life to full-time Christian service. After he had been graduated magna cum laude, he earned a Master of Science degree while teaching three years at the University of Washington. Through his knowledge of engineering and his Christian consecration, he is bringing civilization to his corner of Africa, where thousands of God's children have accepted Christianity.

They have long been told by missionaries that all men are equal in the sight of God. Hal Thwing is helping them to become equal. His work is no less exciting than that of Frank James, the big game hunter, after whom the school was named.

Parts made by this machine make possible the mass production of badly-needed furniture.

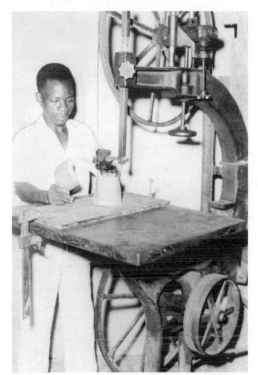

A cottage built by the students. Such houses are being built to replace mud huts all over the French Cameroun by graduates of the school.

under the equator

One day a Michigan farmer set out for Africa. He had studied agriculture. He had had sixteen years of farming experience. He had worked as membership representative for the Michigan Farm Bureau. Now he is an agriculturist, one of the twenty-nine Methodist missionaries working in an area larger than Michigan.

To visit him you would go to Elisabethville in the Belgian Congo under the equator. Nearby is Mulungwishi, with Springer Institute, which has four schools. One school trains teachers; another trains ministers. There is also a school for women and a primary school.

The teachers from here preach, and the preachers teach. Each graduate not only manages both a school and a church but also runs a small demonstration farm.

This area in southern Belgian Congo, the size of Michigan, has two hundred African pastor-teacher-farmers. Ray Smalley, the Michigan agriculturist, says they need twice this number.

Belgian Congo, where Mr. Smalley teaches agriculture, is about the size of the United States east of the Mississippi. It is almost seventy-seven times the size of Belgium, and it is loaded with copper, palm oil, diamonds, and uranium.

You will want Mr. Smalley to tell you about his farming here in Africa.

"There is an ocean of grass here in the Congo," Mr. Smalley says, "which could be turned into milk. Not knowing how to do this, the African burns the grass and with a bow and arrow goes out to hunt for meat."

"Why could not an African out here in the jungle import a good dairy cow from Michigan?"

"That would take ten months of his wages. Even then the parasites and the poisonous weeds might get her. So I am teaching dairying and animal husbandry."

"What about the farmer's tools or machinery?"

"All the tools an African has are a heavy hoe, a hatchet, a knife, an adze, and a spear. We teach him to use a small plow with oxen, or a cultivator, or a cart pulled by donkeys. Soon he sees that this is faster and easier than to dig a field by hand or carry produce and fuel on his head."

"How about the livestock on the school farm?"

"We have fifty-one head of dairy cattle. Ticks and tsetse flies and poisonous weeds make cattle raising difficult. We are trying to overcome these difficulties.

"We are distributing good male goats to the villages. They are increasing the milk supply. We are also distributing improved cockerels and setting eggs to improve poultry."

"What about the crops?"

"When I came here I found two hundred acres of cassava on this school farm. I'm trying to substitute corn mush for cassava mush in the school diet, so I'm raising corn. Cassava is nearly 100 per cent starch. An agricultural missionary in Africa must know something about nutrition, so he'll know what crops to raise. I'm trying to get more protein in the African diet.

"We get protein from peanuts. The women here are learning how to make peanut milk for their children.

"When I came to this school they were buying dried fish to get more protein for the students. This had to be purchased with mission funds. We built a dam, and we are now raising vegetable-eating fish.

"The new dam is being used not only for fish raising but for irrigating our vegetable gardens as well as a grove of 225 citrus fruit trees.

45

"God seems to have plenty of food for his African children if only someone shows them how to produce it."

The mission dispensary here averages fifty-six patients a day. African mothers formerly expected four out of five of their babies to die. Mr. Smalley is trying to change all of this by teaching the people of his larger-than-Michigan-sized area how to raise the proper food.

"Why are such mission schools needed?" you ask.

"In central Africa there is not a single university for 10 million people and hardly a dozen high schools.

"The Governor General of Belgian Congo said, 'It is dangerous to educate Africans. It is much more dangerous not to educate them.'"

This bull was brought in from South Africa to help develop the herd at Springer.

At the school farm, you can see the new hammer mill that Mr. Smalley introduced.

Ordinarily it takes an African wife an hour a day to grind her meal with the traditional mortar and pestle.

The women now come with a week's supply of roots and grains. They dump them into the mill. In a few minutes they have their flour in a sack on their heads and are on their way back home. They have saved seven hours of mortar and pestle pounding. "We try to get them to use this time for improving their home and family life," says Smalley.

"Many of the students come here to school as families. Each student spends twenty-five hours a week in school. Also, he raises part of his food, cooks it, fetches his own wood and water, and takes care of his living quarters.

"The wives go to school four afternoons a week. They study all phases of homemaking. They don't need to borrow any babies to study child care."

You who wear African diamonds must see the hovels in which many Africans live and then for contrast see the homes of these pastor-teachers after their two-year course at Springer Institute. They now have nice, clean rooms with bright curtains, new wicker chairs, and neat beds.

Why did Ray Smalley leave Michigan and go to a place like Africa?

46

"One day in Ag College I was wondering what I was going to do with my life," he explains. "I attended a meeting at which the speaker was asked 'How should a young man decide on his life work? What is the call of God?'

" 'It is seeing a need,' the speaker explained, 'and feeling that in some way you can meet that need.' "

This turned Smalley toward Africa.

Contour farming, illustrated above, enables African farmers to get a better yield from their land. At left, Ray Smalley meets a trusting friend in the field.,

something new in missions

What's new about missions?

You think you've known about missions all your life. You have known that missionaries have been sent out. They make converts, build churches, hire preachers, start schools, equip hospitals. What's new about that?

But there really is something new about missions. Come along to Kambini in Africa and see for yourself.

You land at Kambini, in southern Mozambique, a Portuguese province, way down in southeastern Africa. You're about as far from home as you'll ever get.

You meet Julian Rea, the agricultural missionary here. He is a man in his fifties, from Massachusetts State College of Agriculture. He once taught vocational agriculture a brief period in Georgia.

"What do you have here that we can see in one day?" you ask Mr. Rea.

Students in the elementary classes of Kambini school are alert, attentive, and eager to learn.

"One day!" The thirty long years he's given to Kambini flash across his mind. He remembers that there were the Keys from Kansas Ag and the Gillets from Oregon Ag here before him.

"Well, we've a fifteen-hundred-acre school farm here where we educate the whole family at one time," he replies. "Our total enrollment of men, women, and children is over a thousand."

"Why teach agriculture to women and children?" you ask.

"Farming in Africa has been woman's work since time began," Mr. Rea explains.

"It's the woman with the hoe here in Africa. She does the farming. She cooks the meals and cares for the family."

"What do the men do?"

"They go away to work in the mines occasionally: that is, whenever a famine or drought strikes, and that's plenty often. But when at home, the man is on vacation. Man in Africa, you know, is a superior something-or-other.

"Fathers sometimes send their sons away to school. They like to have them work for the government, or be teachers or preachers, paid from some hidden treasure box, like the mission, for example. There was a Santa Claus era in missions, you know. We've passed that period. Our graduates from Kambini go out to be self-supporting preacher-teachers, and they farm enough to raise their own food.

"On our school farm here the whole family gives half time to school work and the other half to farm work for three years. Our fifteen hundred acres are divided into family plots. Each new family moves in where a graduate has moved out. Each family raises its own food, according to a farming plan we've worked out over a thirty-year period."

49

Two stages in the process of spinning, one of the practical skills taught at Kambini Training School.

"What do you mean by a farming plan worked out over a thirty-year period?" you ask.

"Our farm program, which we've worked out during the last thirty years, includes three main crops," Rea explains, "cowpeas, Kansas corn, and Georgia peanuts. Two of these are legumes. The cowpea vines, the dried peanut plants, and the cornstalks are plowed under to put humus back into the sandy loam.

"In January the students plant their peas and peanuts. In March they chop under the pea vines for green manure. Then we plant corn. Every student's home has a lawn of sweet potato vines and a garden.

"Each student raises his own food and cooks it. He makes his own furniture and often weaves his own clothes. Some of them build their own houses. We've had men here weaving and even making dresses for their wives."

"What's the idea?"

"Each one goes back to his village to be a teacher-preacher and farmer, all three at the same time. Our graduates don't wait for their people to

At far left, a student at Kambini Training School is shown weaving a carpet. At left, a preacher-teacher-to-be is husking corn on the school farm.

build a parsonage for them. They build it themselves, and they know how to build churches.

"They are the best farmers in their communities. Their farms and their homes become demonstrations. They pass on improved seeds to their neighbors, along with their Sunday sermon. They teach the village school. They are self-supporting and are demonstrating a better way of life."

"This doesn't seem like a very difficult job," you remark.

"Well, you should have been here when we started," Rea says.

"It wasn't so easy as you think to change the customs and beliefs of centuries. The African lord and master of the house didn't believe he should go to the field with a hoe and dig just like a woman, and he said so. Those days were rugged for me."

"What happened?"

"I had a saddle mule. He helped me be in two or three places at once, supervising the students.

"When things got too discouraging, I would stop in at the house and ask my wife Mary for a cup of tea. What I really wanted was a little

51

solace. Mary has been my fellow traveler for better or for worse on my African journey.

"Not only did we run into age-old customs we wanted to change, but we ran into the devil at every turn. Africa was full of devils. There was a devil for every disease, every misfortune, every bad crop, every fear.

"So to build enthusiasm for our new farm program, we invented a new devil. 'Famine,' we called him. We added horns and a tail. Famine had all the earmarks. The students understood it through our visual education. They saw how its fierce and fire-eating breath blasts Africa. They would shoot it full of arrows. Each arrow was a feature of our better farming program.

"The students in their classes also were soon writing and depicting plays showing the new pattern of living.

"Perhaps you'd like to hear the characters in one of these plays:

"Mr. Set-in-his-ways and his wife, Lazy; Mr. Good-farmer and his wife, Clever; the Judge; the Year and all his twelve children, the Months; Prince Yellow Corn; Mother Cassava; Auntie Sweet Potato; Miss Rice; Br'er Pumpkin; Bean Legume; Peanut; the Court Jester, who turns out to be the hero; Conscience; Hoe; the Court Police and Sheriff.

"The plays are seldom written. The students practice with the ideas and leave the actual speech form to the inspiration of the hour. This makes it more spontaneous.

"The basic teachings of one of these plays was written in the Xitswa language, our local dialect here. It has gone through two editions and has been used in much of southeast Africa. Some of the characters almost become known by their play names."

"What does all this have to do with the gospel?"

52

"Well, before this, many had become church members. They'd accepted the Christian doctrine. Some had even become ministers, but they were still dominated by their old customs, their old fears, their old attitudes, their old diseases.

"Those who have learned the Kambini plan in their fields and in their homes have really changed their way of life. This is part of conversion. Kenyon Butterfield, my president at Massachusetts College of Agriculture, used to tell us that. He got me interested in agricultural missions.

"I'm confident that at least 90 per cent of those who follow the Kambini plan in their fields and in their homes are better Christians. And approximately 20 per cent of the whole population of our five Methodist Conference areas in Africa are now Christians.

"You see, we try to connect the farm work and the home life with the gospel we preach.

"Our Seed Consecration Service here in our big Kambini stone church might show you what I mean. When the planting rains come, for which both Christians and non-Christians have prayed, our pastor calls the people to evening prayers. All come with their hoes and seed.

"After proper ceremony the hoes and seed are placed on the altar of our great Kambini church and left there for the night.

"At sunrise all are praying again in the church. Then they start singing 'Hoes we bring, Lord, to thee—Bless them! Seeds we bring, Lord, to thee—Bless them, etc.'

"Then they take their hoes and seed from the altar and go forth to plant, with the Lord of the Harvest."

"Do they forget the Lord of the Harvest if they have a good crop?"

"No, they always have a thanksgiving service at harvest time.

"Our church is then turned into a garden. The columns bear huge bunches of coconuts. Young tasseled corn springs out from the altar rail. Sheaves of rice and complete banana plants, with a giant bunch of fruit, are there.

"The climax comes when the choir starts chanting 'Corn we bring, Lord, to thee.'

"Husband starts the procession up the aisle. He lays his big three-bushel bag of peanuts on the altar.

"Wife follows close behind. She has a gasoline tin full of corn balanced on her head.

" 'Corn we bring, Lord, to thee,' the choir continues to chant.

"Children follow with an offering, a bundle of beans, a chicken, or eggs or fruit.

"The choir keeps chanting. One of the chickens is usually sacrilegious enough to gobble up some of the sweet kernels of Kambini corn.

"Now Mother, free of the load on her head, pauses to make Baby, tied on her back, leave his offering.

"Your hearts would probably warm within you, as ours do, as we sense their joyful sacrifice."

Your day is ended. You are ready to leave Kambini. Yes, this religion is down to earth, as Rea says it is. There *is* something *new* in missions—the training of voluntary farmer-preacher-teachers for villages over much of Africa.

This type of agriculture is lifting people heavenward.

53

from rum farm to Christian community

Thirty years ago a two-thousand-acre farm in Mozambique raised sugar cane to be made into rum. Its Indian owner and his numerous wives and half-caste children made a fortune. Then his business was outlawed.

Reeds filled the swamp and river bed. Dense forests smothered the fields. Those who formerly cultivated the cane fields or drank the rum went off to the Transvaal to work in the mines. Family life sank to a new low. This section of the Dark Continent became darker than usual.

Then came a Methodist missionary from Oberlin College, Ira Gillet. His twelve years here at Guilundo Farm has wrought miracles. But you must see it for yourself.

Mr. Gillet is seated on the veranda of his brick house. He burned some of the brick himself. Unhewn eucalyptus pillars cut from the farm hold the screening around the veranda. Just outside is a pink rose watered from the eaves. Farther out is a bright red bougainvillaea. Beyond that a pomegranate. Under the limbs of a tangerine and a mango in bloom on one side and a palm-filled coconut on the other side, you see several papayas. Also, a peach and a lemon tree catch your eye just at the corner.

Across the scene go six women and a man in single file. They are enroute to the village of Chief Guilundo who lives just across the stream, where Manuel, the son of a local Portuguese carpenter by a native wife, is taking the ten-year census. This census will show that there are thousands of Christians in the colony as a result of the work of Mr. Gillet and his colleagues.

"What changes have you noticed, Mr. Gillet, since you came to Guilundo twelve years ago?"

"When Edith and I came, this house was ready to move into, except it had no doors, windows, veranda, ceiling, or screens. The broken cement floor was littered with rusty rum stills.

54

An overloaded basket brings one of life's small tragedies to a child in Mozambique.

"We sawed the lumber from our eucalyptus trees; we burned a kiln of brick.

"Where you see all those homes along the river, there was nothing but a swamp. We drained that. We'll soon have a hundred families there.

"You can't see some things," Mr. Gillet explains. "My field covers an area larger than the state of New Jersey. Our church membership is increasing 18 per cent a year. But you really can't see much of our work.

"Just across the river the chiefs, pastors, and evangelists have formed an agricultural association. They help one another in times of need. You should visit one of the farm fairs organized by them.

"Some years we have as many as four farm fairs in as many regions of this district. They are always set up by local intersociety committees. People come from fifteen miles around, bringing their produce on their heads.

"You can see the exhibits and the crowd of fifteen hundred people and hear their program, but there are many things you cannot see, such as the months of sweat in the cotton and peanut fields, the sorrowful losses of domestic animals, the anxious upward look for God's rain, the often hungry stomachs with blood and intestines full of parasites. Then, here

This small boy seems to be deeply interested in the new methods that are assuring a better future for him and his friends.

they are at their annual fair. A big banner says 'The Earth is the Lord's.'

"Whatever they may be doing, we try to teach them that God is relevant. We want them to remember the spiritual significance of everyday work.

"Since religion has to do with all of life, we might call Guilundo a school for life. Instead of poverty, leprosy, tropical ulcers, we have new potatoes, green peas, cauliflower, papayas, and spinach."

You know more about business than about this type of work, so you ask Mr. Gillet if this farm is self-supporting.

"Most of the things we raise we don't sell. We plant perhaps one thousand coconut trees a year; then we sell our small coconut trees at four cents each in order to get them growing on every farm around here. But we don't sell our music, drama, hygiene, games, or our village crafts. We don't sell our daily classes in religion, or our 4-H Club work. Each year we distribute some forty dollars' worth of garden seeds.

"We are training entire families under rural conditions to go back to the reserves and live. We have made this swamp into a garden. This type of thing must be done all over Africa.

"The forces are here. You see that small electric plant. It generates native power. We had no running water when we came, except as a boy ran down to the river for it.

"The water is here, the same as the electricity, the same as the abilities of the African. Our job is to develop native powers."

You will not easily erase from your mind the church service. They are meeting under a cashew tree. The table upon which the communion elements sit is made of unpolished teak. The chair on which Mr. Gillet sits is mahogany, not veneer, but all solid stuff. Sitting on one side on mats or on the ground are some seventy-five women and girls. No two of their print blouses and colored headcloths are alike. All are clean. Rows of feet, all innocent of shoes, are pointed toward the front.

On the men's side an equal number of men and boys have found for themselves logs, bark, and bundles of reeds for seats.

When the moment comes to kneel at the altar, they come forward to lines marked in the sand. They present cupped hands into which is put the bread. Their hands are thick with callouses made by the bush knife and the short-handled hoe. Your hands are white and soft and feel lazy in comparison.

Then there follows a series of grateful testimonies as to what the Christian gospel means to them and to their neighbors at Guilundo Farm.

a trip up the Nile Valley

Egypt is a strange old land. Flying over it you see the long, narrow, green Nile Valley about fifteen miles wide near Cairo but only two miles wide farther up the stream. North of Cairo the river spreads out into a triangular delta. On both sides of the valley the land is desert. If you include Egypt's two deserts, the country is almost half again as large as Texas. If you omit them, the green Nile Valley where people live and crops grow is only the size of Maryland. Some say this Nile Valley is the most densely populated farm land in the world, with as many as three persons per acre.

When your plane is halfway up the Nile Valley, you land near Assiut College. Here you meet Robert Turnbull, who is in charge of the Department of Agriculture. Mr. Bob, as his Egyptian colleagues usually call him, is nearly six feet tall, has light brown hair, and weighs around 170 pounds.

He is from Penn State College and was sent here by the United Presbyterian Church. He says he already thinks of Egypt as home.

"Egypt is an agricultural country with many people and little land," he begins.

"The valley of the Nile, spread out before you, has some of the richest land in the world. Cotton is the big cash crop. Egyptian cotton is known all over the world for its fine quality and long staple."

"Then I suppose your farmers here are quite prosperous," you remark.

"Just the opposite," he says, as he starts to show you around the campus with its 880 students.

"Cotton is a very speculative crop. One is never sure of a good crop because of disease and insects, nor is one ever sure of the world market price."

"What do you advocate to substitute for it?"

Feeding a few of the thousands of Leghorn chicks that have been brought to Assiut College by the mission in cooperation with the Point Four Program.

"We emphasize a more balanced agriculture. Don't put all your eggs in one basket. Egypt has a climate and soil that would support a large dairy industry. We tell them that dairying and cotton could complement each other. Cotton depletes the soil, while manure from cattle would add to the fertility. Egypt imports hundreds of thousands of dollars worth of dairy products and at the same time imports approximately 15 million dollars worth of commercial fertilizers. Milk products are available only to the wealthy, because of the high price. Milk is not in the diet of the children of Egypt. We agricultural missionaries are fighting for the children, especially the children in the poorer homes."

"Don't you have cows in Egypt?" you ask.

"Yes, but they are used principally as draft animals. They give barely enough milk to feed their calves."

By this time you reach Turnbull's Jersey herd, a hundred head of Jerseys and Grade Jerseys.

"This is our prize cow. We call her Cora. Her great-grandmother was a native cow that gave an average of two thousand pounds of milk per lactation. Cora, who descended from this native cow, in her first lactation period as a two year old gave nearly six times as much."

Somebody who doesn't know much about farming asks what makes the difference.

"It was Jersey blood introduced by Jersey bulls. They passed on an inheritance for milk production. We've found that a one half Jersey cow will give twice as much milk as her native mother."

"Do you have enough cases to prove these facts?" someone asks.

58

Here Bob takes you into the dairy barn and shows you the records. Thirteen mature Egyptian cows, carefully selected for dairy characteristics, averaged 3,032 pounds of milk per lactation. Thirteen half Jerseys averaged 5,437 pounds. Three fourths Jerseys averaged 5,790 pounds and high fraction Jerseys averaged 6,642 pounds.

"When did you start this dairy project?" you ask.

"I didn't start it. Milo McFeeters, my predecessor, brought out three purebred Jersey heifers and one bull in 1928. In 1937 he imported others. He is responsible for the one-hundred-head herd that you see."

"What are you doing that's new?" you ask Professor Turnbull.

"We're carrying on a fairly good extension program. It doesn't help much if we keep all our cows as well as our ideas here on the campus.

"Through the years we have sold about two hundred head of Jersey bulls and part Jersey cows to all parts of Egypt as foundation stock for improved dairies. This project has grown up on a basis of self-support. But two years ago a couple of men from the Ford Foundation visited us. They urged that we should speed up and greatly expand our extension service, and they offered a grant to finance such an enlarged program. So we have now rented an additional farm on a long-time lease. It is some distance south of Assiut and is surrounded by twenty farm villages.

"We've set up four bull stud centers where service from a good purebred Jersey bull is available for just twelve cents. We're convinced that a dairy industry can prosper in this country if we can teach the farmer to own more productive cattle and to feed for production.

59

Bob Turnbull and a coworker are proud of Cora, their prize cow, who plays an important role in supplying better nutrition for Egyptian children.

"For winter forage we raise alfalfa and good Barseem clover. These two crops put organic matter and nitrates back into the soil. We have actually found that two acres with dairying will produce as much as three acres without dairying, and that means a lot in this land-hungry country. The Barseem thrives only through the cooler weather but produces five successive crops. The alfalfa grows the year round and produces twelve crops. For summer feed the Egyptians have mostly depended upon dry, chopped straw with just enough grain mixed in to keep their animals alive, so of course in summer they get no milk at all.

"According to this system we have developed, they can have good and abundant green feed all year round. From spring to fall we make successive small plantings of corn for green fodder. During the summer we raise two enormous crops of fodder on the same land that produced the five cuttings of Barseem during the winter. Along with the corn fodder we feed some alfalfa; also, to the heavy milk producers, a home-grown grain mixture of wheat bran, ground corn, and cottonseed meal.

"We are interested in other farm livestock too. Last year, in cooperation with Point Four of the American Government, we brought in three thousand Leghorn chicks, which we distributed to the farmers. This spring we flew in from Holland some Khaki Campbell duck eggs. Our ducks stand disease better than chickens and now lay between 75 and 80 per cent every day. Soon we will bring in some milk goats from Switzerland to improve the native goats. Many an Egyptian family, too poor to own a cow, has a goat or two. With the help of the United States Department of Agriculture we are also making trial plantings of many kinds of improved seeds."

60

As you leave Assiut College and Bob Turnbull, he thanks you for coming, and says, "We surely want your continued interest in our job here. We're trying to serve the farmers of Egypt. Especially, we're trying to serve the youth of Egypt and the church of Christ in this land we love."

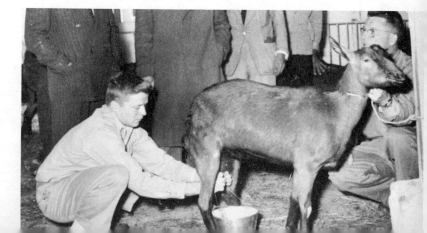

Milk goats from Switzerland help Cora the Cow in the job of supplying milk for better diets.

new cedars for Lebanon

Sitting in a circle on the floor of the Sheik's house in Saboura, a dozen men were talking and eating. Their conversation turned to the subject of schools.

"For boys, yes; but not for girls," said the old Sheik in a guttural voice. "No, if our women become educated we will lose our influence over them."

He tore off a piece of bread, dipped it into the common dish in the center, and went on with the evening feast.

In this village of a thousand people, only five men out of 120 could read and no women. It was time to be talking about schools.

The missionary began talking about a new kind of school for girls. In Saboura 50 per cent of the babies die before reaching the age of five. There is not a glass window in a single house. All the wells are open, and malarial mosquitos are plentiful.

After the missionary had explained it several times, the men fell for it.

"Oh, that kind of a school! Yes, we would like to have our girls get a diploma in cooking and caring for the children, in tending flocks, and in making cakes out of cow dung for fuel."

Finally one day in a Lebanon village, the Jibrail Rural Center was born, with this same missionary, S. Neale Alter, in charge.

Wadad, a teen-age girl in Jibrail, her father, mother, grandmother, and five children lived in one room with no windows. The family cow also shared this room in the wintertime. Wadad became a student at this Jibrail Rural Center.

In this strange school, a pupil advances only to the degree that he improves his home or his village.

Wadad's first assignment was building an outside lean-to for the cow. Then a window was cut in the wall. Then, another room, a screened food

The camel has always been taxi and trolley of the desert. Below, a Muslim woman is shown building her own clay fireplace.

cupboard, a hanging cupboard for clothes, embroidered curtains, even bright cretonne covers for the sofa seat.

Wadad's interest in health and hygiene grew. She is now in her fourth year of nurse's training at the Presbyterian Hospital in Tripoli. Her sister will be graduated this year in home economics at the Jibrail Rural Center.

Mr. Alter can tell us more about this Jibrail Rural Center.

"For twenty years, when I first came to Lebanon," he begins, "I supervised village day schools. The curriculum was imported from America, to which place many of the graduates migrated, leaving behind the same old unsolved problems. Our schools were used by the boys of the more prosperous families as a ladder to climb out of their rural environment.

62

A pretty girl is intent on spinning a perfect pattern as she weaves on the loom at the Jibrail Center.

Left, Neale Alter demonstrates the pruning of olive trees. Right, Mrs. Alter is shown with milk goats imported from Switzerland.

"But the majority were left behind in these villages, handicapped by poverty, disease, ignorance, inferior crops, animals, and implements.

"Many years ago cedars of Lebanon were cut down to build Solomon's temple in Jerusalem and these hillsides were left bare. Our schools had that very same effect on our village life. We need to plant some new cedars on these Lebanon hills."

You notice the Cadillac-camel economy here in Lebanon along the Mediterranean. You see the landowners dressed in French clothes, driving big cars around oriental bazaars and living in big houses in Beirut or Damascus. You see the peasants, on the other hand, driving camels or donkeys to market with meager crops raised on fragmented strips of land

63

Using the celebrated Laubach method, Mr. Alter teaches a village girl to read.

they often do not own. They live in adobe houses, resigned to half income, half happiness, and half living.

"To these peasants," Mr. Alter says, "I have dedicated this Jibrail Rural Center.

"We have classes in agriculture, carpentry, home economics, health, and religion. But a pupil advances only as he puts his new knowledge into use in his home or his village. This same rule applies to the teachers.

"In one of these villages I introduced long-staple cotton seed. It was very successful. The following year many of the people planted it for home use. Soon they found it could be marketed in great quantity. Now they are raising many tons each year.

"That village, which formerly was quite poor, has become prosperous.

"Once, on an extension trip into the sheep-grazing area, I found the sheep dying from anthrax. I helped vaccinate five hundred sheep, with spectacular results.

"Recently we brought in five young Sanaan milk goats from Switzerland. We are introducing milk goats in our villages for the sake of the children's diet."

The program of this Jibrail Rural Center includes both academic and occupational skills. Mr. Alter, the Presbyterian, U. S. A., missionary in charge, came from a Pennsylvania farm home. He, with his colleagues, teaches health and hygiene, agriculture and cottage industries, recreation, and practical religion.

His work on those ancient Lebanon slopes is "to set at liberty those who are oppressed, to proclaim the acceptable year of the Lord."

64

a new nation in an old land

In front of a tent in a Pakistan village a cook is trying to wash the dinner dishes. A young man has come, sits down beside him, and is begging this cook to teach him to read. The cook is supposed to wipe a dish with one hand and point to a word in the Laubach primer with the other hand.

On the far side of the tent stands an automobile with a big sign painted on both sides: "READ. EACH ONE—TEACH ONE."

At the door of the tent a group of people are borrowing books. Evidently they have already been taught to read.

Who are these busy workers who are teaching the people in a hundred villages how to read? What's the hurry? Pakistan is an old land, is it not?

Yes, but it is a new nation in an old land. It was separated from India in 1947 on religious grounds. Five and a half million Hindus and Sikhs left. Six and a half million Muslims poured in, flooding the country with unsettled refugees.

Here begins the story of Laura MacLachlan's literacy program.

At the University of Nebraska she prepared to be a high school teacher. When she was only eight her mother taught her about Paul's call into Macedonia. At twenty-three she left her parents' Eagle Creek livestock farm at Atkinson, Nebraska, in order to serve farm folk in Pakistan. She ran village schools for children and held night meetings for adults.

Then came 1947. The scorched earth policy of the Hindus who left, the bitterness of the Muslims who remained, and the millions of refugees everywhere, compelled this rural evangelist, Miss MacLachlan, to add relief work to her busy program. She was given money to use in making jobs for Christians who were on relief.

"I decided literate people might earn their relief money by teaching others to read," she explains.

"I paid relief teachers a stated amount for each student who passed

Miss MacLachlan is shown beside the car in which she travels among a hundred or more villages securing and training teachers. On one side, in Urdu, are the words that are given in English on the other, "Read. Each One —Teach One."

an examination in the first primer. That was a larger sum than for the succeeding books, which were easier. Soon the community as a whole wanted to learn to read.

"When the relief funds ran out, a few teachers carried on without pay. At first I had only four villages with literacy classes. Six years later hundreds of villagers wanted these classes. Illiterate adults, and they are about 90 per cent of our Christian community, were reading the *Gospel of John* in two months after the first lesson."

First when Britain left, and in 1947 when the Hindus who had held many important jobs left, the Pakistanis had to rise to the occasion. Interest in learning to read and to write was also much increased among the almost half-million Christians in Pakistan.

By 1951, the United Presbyterian Mission asked Miss MacLachlan to give all her time to literacy work. She is also chairman of this work for the other missions throughout Pakistan.

She hires literacy teachers who are trained and experienced. She has an organizer who gets the classes started. She runs schools for training literacy teachers. In her many centers she establishes libraries.

"There are approximately fifty different small books and bulletins, including twenty primers, available for new literates to read," she says. "We need dozens of books or bulletins on practical subjects. We have capable translators."

And then she mentions some of these much-needed practical subjects— legumes, crop rotation, rust and its prevention, drainage, fertilization, animal husbandry, poultry, wheat diseases.

66

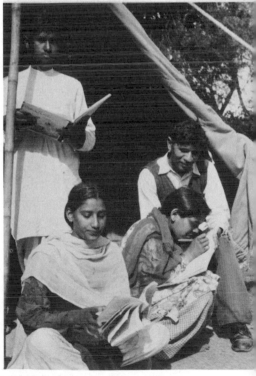

A cook manages to dry dishes at the same time that he is teaching a man to read.

"Send such material at once!" she insists. "Newspapers are not to be had in a rural home. We need scholarship funds to train more literacy teachers. We have the personnel, but no funds with which to pay them."

Americans know too little of this new country of Pakistan, although our two governments have close political ties. With its 76 million people, it is the world's seventh nation in number of inhabitants.

Miss MacLachlan is a capable representative. She says, "An illiterate church cannot become a witnessing church." She and her colleagues are teaching thousands to read.

"In one section," she reports, "if the Christians continue their program to the end of the year, 95 per cent will be reading."

At left, Miss MacLachlan with a Pakistani co-worker, Miss Mabel Massey. Above, the tent library where people who have learned to read may borrow books.

a practical dreamer in the desert

"T he hottest day of my life!" said Friedel Peter and his crew after crossing the Thal Desert through twenty hours of heat and sandstorms.

Perhaps you never saw the thermometer stand at 160 degrees. Mr. Peter and his crew work in that heat. They work at night and try to sleep in the daytime.

They are on the Thal Desert, forty miles from Multan in Pakistan. Friedel A. Peter (pronounced Pater) with a rotary driller is here boring tube wells. In twenty hours he and his crew of workmen sink a well three hundred feet which produces six thousand gallons of water per hour.

Pakistan is a dry and thirsty land. Seventy-two million acres are too high for canal irrigation. The water must be pumped from these irrigation wells.

Take, for instance, the new sugar factory at Mardan. Here's where the government built its big new sugar factory. It was equipped to produce three thousand tons of sugar a day. A huge plant! All the farmers were encouraged to grow sugar cane, which they did. For six months the government tried unsuccessfully to get water for this factory. Mr. Peter, an Episcopalian missionary, drilled and sank a deep well. In two months the sugar factory was running at full speed.

Pakistan has always needed more water. Back in 1947, at the time of Partition, it had a big new refugee problem. Hindus and Sikhs left. The Christians who worked for the Hindu and Sikh farmers were homeless. Muslims poured in. The country was flooded with unsettled refugees.

Mr. Peter first started out trying to help rehabilitate the half million "mass-movement Christians." Technical services is what he calls his work. At first he gave relief employment for a year to five hundred men by digging an irrigation canal. Then he began his well-drilling project.

He employs a crew of twenty men who can sink thirty to forty wells a

68

Pakistanis show deep interest in the plans of missionaries and the United States Government to help them find their place in the sun as they establish a new nation in an old land.

year. Each well can irrigate the land for one new rural village of twenty or twenty-five families.

Two good crops can pay off the debt for the irrigation well. In ten years time the new settlers can own their land with its irrigation system.

This is what Mr. Peter thinks and hopes.

"Rehabilitation is better than charity," is the way he explains it.

"It's the only way to give productive land to these landless people who know nothing but farming," he declares.

You remember the United States Government made a gift of one million tons of wheat to Pakistan.

"Will it be necessary to continue to do this year after year?" is the question Mr. Peter raises. He believes that it will, unless we teach the people how they can help themselves.

"Missionaries have always been pioneers," he points out. "It was the missionaries who built the first schools in all the underdeveloped countries of the world. Now those governments are building schools of their own. Likewise the missionaries pioneered in the field of health.

"Why not pioneer in these much needed technical services?" is Mr. Peter's question.

He is a trained engineer in the employ of the Missionary Society of the Church of England in Canada. His father and grandfather were missionaries to those strange

This farmer smiles as he builds an irrigation ditch to bring water to his farm.

people of Tibet. It was his family who translated the Bible into Tibetan. Now, under the auspices of the interdenominational Christian Council of West Pakistan, he is in charge of what is known as Technical Services.

"A pilot venture" is the term he uses. His first well of 360 feet was completed in ten days, tubing, pump, and all. It would ordinarily take seven months with native equipment.

"The finest equipment in Pakistan" was the way the government referred to his driller. So they loaned him 300,000 rupees to get started. He has repaid this loan on a monthly basis.

Mr. Peter believes that drilling wells for irrigation purposes is the only long-term answer to the problem of settling the half million Christians on the land in Pakistan. The government sells them land under a plan similar to that used by our Farmers Home Administration in America. He hopes eventually to establish small Christian settlements all over Pakistan.

After five years of pioneering he has sold his ten thousand dollars worth of equipment back to the government, and his rotary drill is now being operated by the F.O.A. (Foreign Operations Association).

In this land of almost 76 million people who live on the brink of starvation, Mr. Peter believes missionaries should not say, "We can do nothing about it." And so he is giving his practical help.

The Biblical phrase "water of life" is being given a new meaning in Pakistan through his irrigation wells.

70

One of the hundred refugee women who come each day for the relief and training Miss Peter gives to help rehabilitate them.

Mr. Peter's sister Elsa is caring for a hundred refugee women a day in Lahore. She, too, is helping them to help themselves. She is importing cotton and wool that they are weaving, knitting, and selling to provide food for their families.

She also says that charity has its place, but it is not of the same value as rehabilitation. If you ask Miss Peter how this work is related to evangelism she explains that she has from seventy to two hundred women together every day for five hours, which affords excellent opportunities for classes in literacy and religion.

"I don't need to waste time going from house to house," she explains. "The women come to me of their own accord."

Pakistan has the land, the water, and the people. But they are separated. They are useless until they are brought together. This is one of Mr. Peter's jobs—providing water for men in a thirsty land.

"This," says this practical dreamer, "is part of the task of establishing a self-supporting church in Pakistan."

At far left, Mr. Peter's crew puts in the tubing after a well has been drilled. At left, they test the pump when the well has been completed.

building a backfire against famine

"Yes, in our Vadala section of India we have a famine every six or seven years. Now, we're beginning to feel we're building a backfire against it."

It is Gifford Towle speaking. He's the agricultural missionary at Vadala (Wa-da-la), about two hundred miles east of Bombay.

"Our problem is that we have 361 million people in India in an area approximately the size of the United States east of the Mississippi River. Seventy to 80 per cent of this big population lives on the land and works the land. When the monsoons fail we simply have another famine."

In answer to your question as to what he means by building a backfire against famine, he begins again as he walks toward his deep well with its new diesel pump.

"That's one answer—that diesel pump," he explains. "That cost only five hundred dollars, but it goes farther than that much money put into famine relief funds. That thing pumps 150 gallons a minute.

"When the 1952 famine struck, we put that five-horsepower pump on this bored well and soaked up our fifteen-acre demonstration field. It saved our sorghum crop from total loss and prevented our animals from being sold.

"Our Indian neighbors stood by and watched it work and then asked if we could do that same thing on their fields.

"With the approval of the American Board we bought a second pump. We mounted it on an oxcart, moved it from well to well, and prevented a year's loss of food and income for our neighboring farmers. We charged a farmer three dollars a day for this service, but it soaked up his land and saved his crop.

"We have three of those pumps now.

"The next year, 1953, we had more of the same famine. In the sixty

72

villages where we do extension work there are 128 wells. We offered the owners of these wells black powder, fuse, and crowbars at about half price, and they deepened their wells to strike new sources of water.

"Some of the farmers walked twenty-five to thirty miles weekly to secure powder and fuse. More than half of them struck new and adequate sources of water.

"This is our *bazri,* or sorghum." Mr. Towle points to an irrigated ten-acre field. "It's a grain sorghum, not a sugar sorghum, something like the millet you raise in America. We purchased seven tons of this seed with famine relief funds.

"The farmers had eaten all their seed as well as most of their animals during many days of hunger. We distributed this *bazri* seed to 314 farmers in forty-two villages. Now that the rains have come they have raised approximately seven hundred tons of *bazri* from this seed.

"Our idea is to assist them in helping themselves instead of giving them grain or money to bail them out of dire poverty or hunger.

"Ordinarily we get about twenty-seven inches of rainfall a year. In 1952 and 1953, we got only ten inches. We have a drought every five to seven years. We decided to do a better job of saving the rain we had, so we started contour terracing.

"Our sixty acres, as you see, are all terraced. This sparked the government to try terracing.

"When the 1952-1953 famine struck, the government was looking for work projects to provide people famine relief. We had the farms here surveyed and laid out for terracing. More than five hundred acres were terraced under government supervision. Now we're holding both the soil and the water."

"It could be said, Mr. Towle, that you're beating American swords into Indian plowshares."

"Speaking about plowshares—" and he begins anew.

"We made a survey of three of the sixty villages we serve. We found that the fifty-one farmers in the three villages had 1,111 acres of land. Only 57 of these 1,111 acres were watered from wells. Only one of these fifty-one farmers had a plow.

"The last time I was home I spoke at a church meeting in New Hampshire. That church gave me twenty plows. We have more than fifty now. Some we sell and some we rent. We charge a rental fee of two cents per day. We get the plows made right here in India, at a cost of twenty-five dollars each.

73

"We are developing four extension centers from which we can serve our sixty villages. We keep our plows at the extension centers. We carry on our poultry projects from there. Also, we distribute seeds and insecticides from there. We have introduced soya beans, hybrid corn, Texas sorghums, Louisiana yams, and guinea grass."

"Do you give away setting eggs or cockerels?"

"Neither one," Towle answers rather abruptly. "We don't give away anything, unless it is food in time of famine. India is a proud and self-respecting republic. The give-away program of the American Government has made everybody over here suspicious of America's motives.

These women are winnowing grain in the traditional manner.

"No, we trade either cockerels or setting eggs from our purebreds for the native stock, one for two. We keep from three hundred to five hundred purebred laying hens all the time in order to be able to carry out our plans.

"When we made that survey I told you about awhile ago, we found those fifty-one farmers had a total of only 121 fowl, an average of little more than two per farm."

As you walk about the farm with Mr. Towle, he shows you his sheep, cattle, fruit, and vegetables on the fifteen acres of irrigated land and sixty acres of terraced dry-land fields.

A load of manure being taken to market to sell as fuel. Missionaries are trying to teach the people to use it to enrich the land.

Below, Gifford Towle and an assistant with plow. Mr. Towle has brought in fifty plows, some of which he rents. Bottom right, a diesel pump that pours 150 gallons of water a minute on a thirsty field.

It looks as though he's just a good diversified farmer. Any good American farmer would do it that way, and you tell him so.

"That's right. These Indian farmers expect to earn a year's living by eight or nine months' work, just like our old one-crop American farmers in the South. We're showing them that a year-round income in this area is possible only by diversified full-year farming."

Gif Towle, as he was called back at Massachusetts College of Agriculture, is a good American farmer with a great love for his Indian neighbors. When he attended Mt. Hermon School for Boys, he used to walk four miles across the country to the Northfield School for Girls. Both schools were founded by the contagious religion of Dwight L. Moody. As a result of these trips, one of the Northfield girls, Marjorie Blossom, came to India with him and has helped him spread the Moody type of contagious religion.

His Vadala mission, operated by the Congregational Christian Churches, has six trained pastors and eight lay preachers who serve sixty villages. Twenty primary schools are conducted, which send their most promising students to the Vadala Vocational School of one hundred students. The thirty-five bed hospital and the baby welfare centers take care of health.

Mr. Towle has developed the demonstration farm and the extension program. He has five well-trained Indians working with him in his extension service.

As you prepare to leave Mr. Towle, you want to know why he works so hard for the farmers of these sixty villages.

76

"I'm not interested in agriculture, health, education, or social work as such, alone or separate from the Christian message," he says, "but I'm anxious that the Christian message touch the whole of life here in this one needy section of India."

a new philosophy of education

In the Bombay area of India at Anklesvar (Uncle-es-var) there is a unique Vocational Training College, with eighty-five acres and seventy-five students, where you will be able to see an entire new philosophy of education.

Amsy Bollinger, a slightly bald, middle-aged, agriculturally-trained Indiana farmer, is in charge of the school and is ready to answer your questions.

"How large is your school farm, and what do you do with it, Mr. Bollinger?"

"We have eighty-five acres. Much of it is divided into small plots, which are rented to the students. From the crops each student raises he pays for the rent of his land, his irrigation water, his seeds, as well as a part of his school expenses.

"Often these farm boys enter school without a cent and leave with a diploma and sometimes a small bank account."

"What is this, Mr. Bollinger, that we hear about the white-collar attitude of many students in India?"

"Our school is called the Vocational Training College. Our students deal with the relationships of men, plants, and animals. I think you'll not find any white-collar attitudes here. We call this a life-related curriculum. Let's walk around.

"Here is our carpentry class. This boy is making a yoke for a pair of oxen. That fellow over there is putting a steel moldboard onto an Indian plow. These fellows, as you see, are building furniture. Believe it or not, those boys built one of our school dormitories.

"Before going out on the farm, you must see our younger students. First they grew those vegetables. Now they're drawing pictures of them, measuring them, watering them, weighing them, and they'll sell them and

Amsey Bollinger greets two graduates of the Vocational Training College who now hold important positions as teachers. One is headmaster of the local government school.

keep an account of their income. They're studying arithmetic, drawing, writing, and spelling right here in the garden."

As Mr. Bollinger leads you toward the first field, you pass flaming bougainvillaea, crepe myrtle, hibiscus, and oleander. An oriole is welcoming you with his joyous song.

Mr. Bollinger begins pointing and talking. "This student is plowing under tall hemp for green manure. We find we must teach the boys how to put humus and nitrogen back into worn-out soil. India has been half farmed for centuries.

"What do you think of these white, fluffy bolls of cotton? Those boys will get a yield nearly twice the national average here in India.

"These boys are threshing Kaffir corn, tramping it out with oxen."

"Why don't you use a real threshing machine, Mr. Bollinger?"

"I expected you to ask that," Bollinger answers. "We must train these

78

Near right, hemp is being plowed under as a green manure at the Vocational Training College farm. Far right, Mr. Bollinger and a pastor visit one of the church members in his field of kaffir corn.

boys to live here in India. The per capita income here is only one sixteenth what it is in America. They can't buy your American machines.

"We're reaching a lot of people through this school. We have three departments. You saw our carpentry school. Now, these boys are studying to be farmers. But our main job here is training rural teachers. Our forty students have increased to seventy-five.

"From every section of the farm you can see our church. It's dome can be seen for many miles, and its influence with its 935 members spreads far out into many village areas.

"Our newest addition to the school is a Department of Extension. It's a cooperative venture of five missions. To help me in the extension work, I have an Indian young man with an agricultural degree from Cornell, a young missionary who is a trained engineer, and a woman with special training in literacy methods."

"Who developed the educational philosophy of Anklesvar, Mr. Bollinger?"

"Our Church of the Brethren that started this school always has been fairly close to the soil. Dr. Ira W. Moomaw, now director of Agricultural Missions, Inc., spent nineteen years here. He should have the credit for our Anklesvar philosophy of education.

"Here is our dining room. The students eat the food they have planted, cultivated, and cooked. In a land where the empty stomach is still the greatest obstacle to social progress, mealtime is the best part of our school day."

As you leave Anklesvar you feel that the time is coming when even in India there may be more food and less famine for people who have toiled patiently and long.

79

new farmers on old farms

Old farmers are not always the best. Take India, for example; most of India's land has been farmed for centuries. The land there is worn out. Indian farmers haven't fed their soil. The soil doesn't feed the cows and chickens. The daily output of the cows, the chickens, and the farmers are all low—too low.

For some years, this agricultural situation has challenged the missionaries. In 1911 Sam Higginbottom started to do something about it. He started an agricultural school at Allahabad.

Saskatchewan recently has sent one of its farm boys to Allahabad, India, to help solve this problem. He is Bob Rae, who teaches agricultural engineering at the Agricultural Institute.

80

A missionary instructs students on the school farm.

Bob is the first Canadian to join this team of sixty men who are changing the rural life of India, as well as much of South Asia.

Bob's father is a minister in Vancouver, but it was the six summers on his uncle's farm in Saskatchewan that turned him toward agricultural missions. As soon as he got his M.S. degree in agricultural mechanics at the University of Saskatchewan, he and Mrs. Rae set out for India.

"The program," he says, "is threefold. We teach agriculture to 335 students here on our campus. In our research program we are trying to find the answers to many of the problems facing Indian farmers. Then we carry on an extension program in four hundred Indian villages.

"We offer a two-year course in dairying. India has what are sometimes called sacred cows that wander around, eat off the land, and produce nothing. We're trying to substitute for them good dairy cows that will help feed India's 361 million people. When children are hungry we think a cow that gives milk is more sacred.

"Also, we have a regular four-year course for which we give a B.S. in agriculture.

"There is great need in India for men trained in irrigation, soil conservation, and mechanized agriculture. In 1942 we started a five-year course in agricultural engineering.

"In 1943 the institute began a much-needed two-year course for girls in home economics.

This threshing machine is part of the equipment used at Allahabad to teach young Indian farmers the important know-how of modern mechanized agriculture.

"Our 335 students come mostly from India, but we have a few from Nepal, Burma, Malaya, Ceylon, East Africa, and the Fiji Islands.

"The newest thing around here is our extension program. We have fifty-one extension workers. We call them *gaon sathis,* which means 'village companions.' Each one works in eight to ten villages, including the one in which he lives.

"Here at the school we give six-weeks courses in extension methods. Students come from all over North India for this training.

"A lot of materials must be produced for all this extension work. We make posters, charts, and filmstrips. Every evening we give a fifteen-minute radio program over the All-India Radio."

"How does religion fit into this farm program?"

"All of our students," says Mr. Rae, "receive Christian training as well as technical education. About one third of them are Christians. There is an active Student Christian Movement among them."

"Who supports you and the other sixty teachers?" you ask Mr. Rae.

"The United Church of Canada supports me. In fact, I was the first Canadian on the staff here.

"Nine different denominations are cooperating in maintaining this school and its staff.

"The Ford Foundation is supporting our extension program. There are also some grants from the Indian Government.

82

"We're not only training students to be agriculturists and village workers, but we're trying to train them to be useful citizens in this great new democracy of India."

You recall that in August, 1947, the democracy of India was born. In the winter of 1951-1952, India held her first election, with 107,580,-000 new citizens, both men and women, going to the polls. Thus India took her place as one of the bulwarks for democracy in this new world revolution for freedom for the forgotten millions of Indian peasants.

India, which has followed our trail to freedom, needs our cooperation and help.

Bob Rae, trained on a farm in Saskatchewan and in the University of Saskatchewan, is representing us well in India.

missionaries in feathers

Hungry, scantily-clothed women bending low in the fields, searching for stray heads of wheat or barley! Little girls with big baskets on their hips collecting with their bare hands the manure that falls from the oxen to take home and make cow-dung cakes for fuel! Slender boys whose legs have only shins and no calves! Outcaste fathers trying to support families on wages of two cents a day!

These were mass-movement Christians in India—fifteen thousand of them living in six hundred scattered villages in an area the size of four Ohio counties. To them, over forty years ago, a Presbyterian missionary came to preach the abundant life.

These are the words this missionary, Mr. Arthur Slater, used in describing his people:

"They were downtrodden, fettered, and burdened by debt. They were spending their lives in a wretched striving for food and clothing.

"Their lives were buried in fear—fear of evil spirits, fear of offending the gods, fear of their landlords, and fear of their own religious leaders.

"But most of these villagers kept a few small scrub chickens."

And here begins the forty-two-year story of the missionaries in feathers.

"A men's Bible class in Coatesville, Pennsylvania," Mr. Slater explains, "sent me a pen of twelve magnificent pedigreed Rhode Island Reds. They arrived with the roosters crowing and the hens laying. In two months all of them were dead.

"I learned how to control the tick fever that killed them.

"The men's class sent word saying, 'We're no quitters,' and along came a second lot, better than the first.

"Then Pennsylvania State College sent me one hundred pedigreed White Leghorns. Ontario Agricultural College, my alma mater, sent some fine pedigreed Barred Rocks."

83

Missionaries are always stressing the need for cottage industries or supplementary income. Mr. Slater decided on poultry raising.

"In this Etah District," he explains, "of the six hundred villages, 375 now have purebred fowls.

"This poultry project has spread to three other similar districts, Mainpuri, Etawah, and Farrukhabad.

"From our main farm here and our eight branch poultry farms we distribute cockerels, pullets, and hatching eggs. Each branch farm supplies the needs of approximately twenty villages."

"What has this poultry project accomplished?" you wish to know.

"In the first place, the weight per egg or per fowl has trebled. Many a family is able to double its income by raising poultry. One man is reported to have received the equivalent of eight months' salary in prizes and sales at the big Etah Poultry Show."

"What is this big Poultry Show?"

Mr. Slater's enthusiasm increases as he tells you it is the biggest show in India.

"In 1915, when we had our first poultry show," he explains, "fifty fowls were ex-

hibited. Now the show lasts five days with exhibits running into the hundreds.

"The entire first day is given to penning the fowls. It takes two days to judge them. The prizes are awarded in the afternoon of the third day. The last day is market day, which provides a sale for the fowls that were exhibited."

But you must see the Etah Poultry Show to understand how it has reached down to the poorest laborer and out to the most remote village, how it has built up incomes and broken down castes.

It is the first day of the show. They are coming to pen their fowls. Here comes an Indian pastor who has ridden twenty miles on a bicycle with his basket of purebreds on the front and his wife riding behind. A high-caste Hindu riding on a camel is bringing his exhibits from afar. Twenty years ago he would not have associated with these untouchable farm laborers. From a mud hut village a boy is walking, bringing some birds in a basket on his back. His precious fowls win prizes over those of merchants or landlords. A Muslim woman, reputed to have no soul, has some prize layers. School children come with their

teachers for a five-day lesson in poultry raising. Educated Hindus and illiterate villagers are one, all meeting and eating together for five days.

During these five days there are evangelistic meetings, popular lectures, motion pictures, and demonstrations.

In addition to this big Etah Poultry Show, there are eight smaller shows in the branch stations.

Besides raising poultry, Mr. Slater's farm was the first goat-breeding farm in India. The government now is establishing similar farms.

"I want to see every village have six things," he explains, as he reviews his forty-two years of work in India. "They are a school, a simple church, a dispensary, a resident preacher-teacher, one or more pens of purebred chickens, and improved stud bucks for crossing with country goats."

You ask whether the churches have kept growing along with the poultry project.

"Yes, only more so," he explains. "Through the work of our Indian pastors, I've seen fifteen thousand villagers become Christians in this Etah District. Similar progress is being made in the other three districts."

Before leaving the Etah Poultry Show you must stop for a word with the government poultry specialist who is acting as judge. She is Mrs. A. K. Fawkes, a well-trained Indian woman.

"I have acted as one of the judges at Mr. Slater's big Poultry Show for several years," she explains. "If you had seen these same people ten years ago, when they were really poor and starving, and could see them today, sturdy and independent and keen on this poultry industry, you would be glad you've had a share in Mr. Slater's work."

those who walk alone

A sanctuary of sorrow! Here mothers come to see but not to touch their children. Wives talk with their stricken husbands. Many come, but few leave. To this sanctuary of sorrow Edith Dutton has given twenty-eight years of her life.

"Surely this is not that ancient disease of leprosy?" you ask in a hushed voice.

"Yes, centuries ago the cry of 'unclean, unclean' was raised against the victims of this very disease," she replies.

Miss Dutton is a trained nurse and missionary of the Assemblies of God. She is in charge of this leprosy colony at Uska Bazar in Basti District in North India. She has given her life to "those who walk alone."

You ask Miss Dutton if there are many leprosy victims in the world or if leprosy is only an ancient disease.

"It is estimated that there are from five to ten million leprosy patients in the world today," she says. "They are in every country. They are in greater numbers in tropical or subtropical regions. It has been estimated that only 3 per cent of all leprosy patients in the world today are receiving any medical care."

"What can you do, Miss Dutton, for these unfortunate people?"

"We give injections that arrest but do not cure. We have our fifty-three-acre farm. Our equipment may not be the best. We have two yoke of good oxen, this rubber-tired oxcart, a station wagon, and other farm equipment.

"You can see how busy our people are, planting and harvesting, threshing, grinding, winnowing, and polishing rice.

"Also, we have some poultry. It's very necessary for the patients to have some work to do; it's better that they keep active. The growing crops give them hope.

"When this district suffered a three-year drought from 1947 to 1950, we installed an irrigation pump. If the rains fail now, we can still have a good crop."

When you ask Miss Dutton about her many duties in this self-supporting leprosy colony, she explains, "I have the help of a good Indian pastor and his wife. Between us we manage the farm, the hospital, and the church. But I have to know which type of fertilizer to use, which seeds are the best to plant, and the best way to care for the poultry. I'm the only missionary here, but I'm doing what I want to do."

These leprosy patients are being tranported in a bullock cart.

"I remember that when I was a girl and people would ask me what I was going to be when I grew up, I always said I wanted to be either a nurse or a missionary. Now I'm both. As to the farm, we are here in one of the deficit areas of this great land of famine and drought. The ancient curse of leprosy removes its victims from their families and friends. They must live alone, without friends and without hope. Plowing and planting, harvesting and threshing, bring back hope and faith."

As you leave Miss Edith Dutton and her work in the leprosy colony at Uska Bazar in North India, no doubt you will recall those words spoken so long ago, "Truly I say to you, as you did it to one of the least of these my brethren, you did it to me."

Mr. Bannerjie, pastor, prepares
leprosy patients for baptism.

the village center plan

Mr. Abraham, an Indian teacher in one of the 240 villages around Vikarabad included in John Patterson's Village Center plan, begins the day by taking his school children to a well where they must wash their faces, hands, and legs. He collects two annas a month from their parents to buy the soap.

While they are at the well, Mrs. Abraham is cleaning the schoolroom. When they return, she is waiting at the door with a comb in her hand. She combs the girls' hair daily.

Then classes begin.

Beside the school is the Abraham's new modern four-room house. When they came, only one in seven of the other homes had two rooms. The rest had one room. None had a glass window.

Mr. Abraham also has a big garden. Look at his vegetables: beetroot, beans, cabbage, tomatoes, brinjals, ladyfingers, chilies, and carrots.

"I gave some of these vegetables to my neighbors to taste," he explains.

" 'These are good,' they said. 'Let us grow them, too.' "

90

Near right, a school boy at Vikarabad works in the garden. Far right, Mr. Patterson helps a villager build a mud house.

A committee from an outlying village, driven by a hunger greater than the appetite for food, has come to the mission to ask that a teacher be sent to them.

His flower garden contains crotons, roses, jasmine, marigolds, asters, dahlias, and lilies.

"When these roses are blooming, my garden shines like the sky with stars during the night," is the way he describes it. Not much beauty in his village for comparison, so he uses the sky!

"People come to see my garden every day and enjoy it very much, for they see flowers and vegetables they have never seen before. Most of the people say they are planning to have a garden like it.

"I made brush brooms and taught the people to sweep their yards. Also, I taught them how to build compost pits and use manure on their fields.

91

Each village center has a pastor, a teacher, and a nurse. In this picture, a village center nurse is showing the newest baby.

"My wife and I conduct an evening class for the women in canning and sewing. On special days, such as Christmas and Easter, the people whitewash their houses."

Mr. Patterson, who heads up the Village Center plan, is a Methodist missionary from Kansas. Baker University, Kansas wheat farms, and Drew Theological Seminary prepared him for rural work in India.

When you read about more than 600,000 villages in India, you wonder how the missionaries can serve so many people. Mr. Patterson's Village Center plan at Vikarabad is one answer.

In this rural town of fifteen hundred people there is a coeducational school of six hundred pupils and a twenty-bed hospital. Pastors, teachers, and nurses are trained here.

Around the town of Vikarabad there are sixteen Village Centers. In each of these is an Indian pastor, a teacher, and either a nurse or a compounder. In each there is a church, a school, and a health clinic.

Surrounding each of the sixteen Village Centers there are about fifteen smaller villages or subcenters served by the pastor, the teacher, and the nurse from the Village Center.

In the subcenters or smaller villages there is usually one village worker, like Mr. Abraham, who runs a day school for the children, a night school for the adults, and also a Sunday school.

92

While touring the villages, Mr. Patterson sleeps and eats in a tent. He is shown here enjoying what he calls a "private" lunch.

Most of the people in this Vikarabad area are farmers, averaging 5.1 acres per family. A few of them are shoemakers, and a few others are day laborers.

Every third family has a buffalo and a goat. One family in eight has a sheep.

Taxes amount to one third of the annual income. The average family is in debt two and a half times its annual income.

The families have lost a third of their children, most of whom died under three years of age.

In order to improve the lot of Indian Christians, Mr. Patterson has developed this Village Center plan. He uses thirty pastors and teachers to carry his program to the 240 villages. In his district there are eighteen thousand Christians who look to him for the more abundant life. He brings his pastors and teachers in to Vikarabad for short courses, and he takes his middle school pupils out to the villages for supervised field work.

Mr. Patterson is different from a government worker sent out by Point Four. He knows the language, lives with the people, has been in Vikarabad twenty-seven years, and trains his own workers for the 240 villages. In contrast, a government man lives in the city, drives out to the country in an automobile, speaks through an interpreter, and usually returns to America after two years or less.

Both are helping the underdeveloped countries of the world. The government man is trying to "fight communism" and "win friends for democracy."

Mr. Patterson says his work is "an expression of Christian love as an aid in preaching the good news of God's kingdom on earth."

93

A typical outdoor preaching service. The accommodations may not be luxurious, but wholehearted interest abounds.

a man without caste

Maurice is sitting on a rope cot on Ram Dayal's choupal. A choupal is a raised mud platform where Ram does his carpentry work. As Maurice and Ram talk, the neighbors gather round. They come mainly to listen, although they appear busy, smoking their hookahs.

"Who are you?" they ask Maurice.

"I'm a village worker in extension service from Ingraham Institute," he says.

"What caste are you?" they ask, as they puff away.

"I'm a Christian. We Christians don't believe in caste. We're all brothers."

"Very strange! Are you a teacher?"

"Yes," says Maurice, "I'm a teacher and a learner at the same time. How many of you can read and write?"

"I can," says Ram, "but the headman of our village can't even sign his name."

You are told later that Maurice got Ram to teach a literacy class here, using the Laubach method.

Maurice goes for a parcel from his bicycle and comes back with two wheat plants. On one there are thirty large kernels of grain and on the other five.

"This one is Punjab 591," he says.

By this time their curiosity gets the better of them, and they begin to ask questions.

"Is the little head from India and the big one from America?" they ask.

"No, these were both raised right here in India." Then he explains about seed selection, about the new steel moldboard plow, about green manure, and about compost pits.

The men puff, and they think. It's too much for them. Finally one says,

94

Students learn a useful trade in the tailoring class of Ingraham Training Institute. It will help bring security to them and their families.

"Suppose we had good seed like that—the rains might not come! The seed might spoil before the time to sow it."

Maurice goes back to his bicycle for another parcel, this time for some gammexene, an insecticide, which he has persuaded the local shopkeeper to sell.

By this time the crowd has grown and includes women and children. The women have their faces covered. They are still in purdah.

Ram explains that his only baby died of tetanus shortly after birth four months ago. He and his family live in a two-room mud house and a courtyard. There are no water, no bathing nor latrine facilities. Maurice knows that tetanus comes from filth, and he asks about the use of soap.

"We can't afford soap," Ram explains, as he tells how his father died a year ago when his head was crushed at a sugar-cane mill, how his mother was left for him to care for, how his brother died of sunstroke, leaving a young wife and a three-year-old girl and another baby on the way, and how he, Ram, had to support them all, poor as he is.

"But you aren't too poor to plant castor beans, are you?"

You learn later that Maurice showed them how to make soap from the castor beans they raised.

Each time Maurice goes to his bicycle to get something, he wades through a muddy lane. And for every trip, Ram remarks, "I must make a ditch to carry that water away."

95

"That will merely carry it away to someone else's door," Maurice says. The men nod. They recall that there have been lawsuits in that village over lesser things.

Trim rows of student dormitories typify the planned orderliness and efficiency of the institute's program.

"Let's dig a soakage pit," says Maurice. "If we all work it will take only a short time."

As the men dig, the women peek from under their veils. The children scurry around the lanes, getting broken bricks and bits of clay jars to fill in the hole. Just as Maurice said, soon the *soakta* is made.

As you return to Indergarhi, the village in which Maurice and his wife live, you ask more about this village service.

"I find myself very happy in this type of work," he explains.

"My work is to talk to village people about the everyday needs of their family, flock, or field: the need for water, the cause and cure of sickness, all the ramifying facts about changing to improved seed. We discuss how to keep their village clean when all the land is flat alluvial soil with drainage almost impossible.

"Poverty and caste have reduced community consciousness to a minimum. The Indian farmer is never sure he can make both ends meet; he has worked too long using less and less land.

"When we establish a relationship as brothers, then and not until then are we able to discover needs that the Indian himself feels.

"We help build wells with washing places for the family laundry and floors for washing animals. We help organize credit unions, consumers' societies, literacy committees.

"We have twenty wheat demonstration plots and also a purebred Jersey bull. Much of our work is with kitchen gardens.

"I have eight students working with me. They are learning to be village workers. Our literacy classes average fifteen people each. We have at-

96

Instructors and students utilize what they have and acquire new equipment as they are able. Water buffaloes furnish a milk supply, and fruits are saved by canning to enrich scanty diets. The institute has introduced the steel moldboard plow to the area it serves.

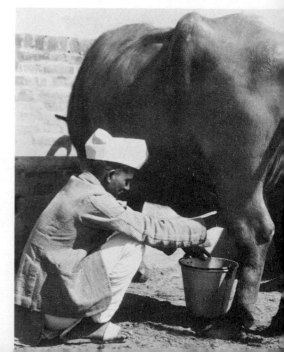

tained 40 per cent literacy in our village. We look forward to the time, perhaps in two more months, when we can point to an even higher percentage of literacy in some of the other villages.

"The government is pushing this extension work all over India, looking forward to having one Indian extension worker for every five villages. This is a part of what is called India's Six-year Plan.

"We missionaries are helping by training personnel and providing the dynamic. Of course the Indians are better extension workers than we are. We have a chance here to live out our faith in action."

The work of Maurice Sill is called extension work or village service.

His father was a county agricultural agent back in West Virginia and later in Pennsylvania. His mother was one of the pillars of the church. The influence of his family and his four years at Penn State College sent Maurice Sill to India as an agricultural missionary.

He works at a Methodist school at Ghaziabad, called Ingraham Teachers' Training Institute. This is one of the most grass-roots, down-to-earth schools in India. For too long, the white-collar disease has attacked many students in India, but not at Ghaziabad.

Before going to India, Maurice Sill was active in 4-H Clubs, the Future Farmers of America, the Methodist Youth Fellowship, and in summer camps. You who are still active in these organizations should visit Maurice and learn what a Christian county agent does in Indian villages.

Agricultural Missions, Inc., says a thousand more agriculturally-trained young men, like Maurice, are needed for this type of work in the fifty underdeveloped countries of the world.

97

I stay in village work

Charlotte Wyckoff arrived in India in 1893, weighing only seven pounds. When she grew up, her missionary parents sent her home to Northfield and to Wellesley.

When she returned, she taught in a Girls' High School for twenty-five years before she had a chance at village work.

"I was shocked and grieved by the state of poverty and ignorance of the village people," she reports. "This was the first chance I'd had to go into the villages and to see something of rural life and its problems in India. I volunteered for rural work, but it was ten years before the Mission Board of the Reformed Church could get someone to take over the Girls' High School.

"It was in January, 1941, that I pitched my tent under a banyan tree. With an Indian helper, I tramped from village to village pursuing adventures in friendship.

"Like a busy spider, I tried to weave the various threads together into a pattern of life more abundant for the villagers and their children."

After thirteen years, she has a busy colony of thirteen Indian workers on three different sites a quarter of a mile apart.

The whitewashed church with a tile roof is at the center. There are approximately nine hundred Christians in this and fourteen other neighboring villages.

Her Indian-size farm, 5.3 acres, serves as a center for agricultural extension with purebred poultry, modern steel plows, irrigated gardens, and fruit. The calendar in this section of rural India now includes such events as Adult Education Week, Grow-More-Food-Week, Tree-Planting Week, and Compost-Pit Week.

Each morning nearly two hundred boys and girls walk in from thirty-three villages, generally with empty stomachs, and attend sixth-, seventh-, and eighth-grade classes.

There is a nursery and kindergarten where sixty or seventy children can have that strange experience among underdeveloped countries—a secure childhood—with baths, naps, play, stories, songs, games, clean water to drink, and clean habits.

The village handicrafts school, the other adult classes, the evangelistic work, and the dispensary complete the services of Miss Wyckoff's rural center, which is known as Jothy Nilayam, meaning "Abode of Light."

During the rainy season, the front porch of the Hill Memorial Church is covered with a pavilion of flowering creepers. The verse above the door says, "Christ is the Way, the Truth, and the Life."

Other Americans touring India stop off at the cities, but usually miss the 600,000 villages. But you are not going to miss Miss Wyckoff's village of Muttathur. The only things large about it are the mountains of poverty, ignorance, and superstition. Here you will understand rural India.

While here, you learn that for each airplane like yours flying across India there are ten thousand bullock carts and country buses traveling along the country roads.

You learn that 85 per cent of the country's population live by a primitive method of agriculture depending largely on the weather. When you see the results of their unscientific methods, you understand why the people personify the elements as well as their diseases as demon-goddesses.

Here comes a procession now. The villagers have made an effigy of Kodum Pavi, the demon who seems to personify the hostile elements that prevent rain. They are parading around the village beating and kicking this poor clay figure. At last they throw it out on the rubbish heap.

"No matter which god we worship," they cry, "with processions, with festivals, rockets, offerings! —none hears! none answers! and none cares!"

The happy optimism of this young mother shows in her face as she arrives at the dispensary with her young child.

During the last five years of drought Miss Wyckoff has dug new wells and deepened old ones in order to irrigate the fields in her section.

You visit her Gruel Center, to which come people in rags and tatters, gaunt and apathetic with long undernourishment or ravenous with hunger. During the drought she fed bowls of gruel to as many as six hundred in a single day.

You watch the young mothers who have their last shreds of cloth pinned together with thorns. Their children are naked or in rags and are always hungry. Miss Wyckoff mixes the powdered milk that American women have sent her and during the famine cares for as many as a thousand of these in one day.

But there are others you see, such as the stalwart young farmers and artisans who have been graduated from her school. Then there are full-fledged teachers who have started schools of their own, who came to her first as herdboys from her thirty-three villages. You may not see all her graduates, since some are away in college. She has opened the windows for them into a new world.

Every day seems to be a special day here. The Leprosy Clinic is held on Tuesdays and Fridays, under government auspices. Seven hundred leprosy patients are on the roll now for injections, and more are added each week. On one day one hundred patients had cataracts removed between 7 A.M. and 7 P.M. by a team that came from the Christian Medical College at Vellore. Not bad for a thatched-roof dispensary!

"Do you tire of other people's needs?" you ask Miss Wyckoff.

"When I must go away on mission business I welcome the change, but I find my heart lifting noticeably when I climb into the home-coming bus and again come in sight of the Gingee Hills and then Muttathur.

"Although seven buses pass this village daily, it is not on any map except the ones our school children draw for their class in home geography.

"I always tell our people here not to thank me, but to thank God.

"They say, 'Missie, you are all that we know about God.'

"And so I stay in village work."

a mission station with four sides

A plow is being used as a pulpit. The De Valois Memorial Chapel is decorated with grains, fruits, vegetables, and flowers—all products of the farm and garden. The architecture of the chapel is Indian. It has twenty-six pillars on which are carved nineteen crosses and many Christian emblems, as well as symbols of farm and field.

Behind the plow-pulpit, which is garlanded with fruits and flowers, an Indian bishop is preaching. He speaks of farming as a partnership with God. It is annual Rural Life Sunday at the Katpadi Agricultural Institute in India. Laymen from a hundred Christian villages are present.

The chapel is open on three sides, thus giving expression to the universal invitation, "Come to me, all who labor and are heavy-laden, and I will give you rest."

"Heavy-laden?" Yes, heavy-laden. Hunger lives with many and threatens many more. We read that "life begins at forty," but here in India it ends at twenty-seven, for that is the life expectancy in this land of 361 million people. But twenty-seven years is a long time to live if one is hungry. The Agricultural Institute at Katpadi is doing much to remedy this situation in South India where two million Christians live.

101

The next visit to Katpadi is on the last day of the fair. For three days ten thousand Indian farmers have been living in a fresh new world. There are mangoes, limes, oranges, and other fruits. There are Scindhi cows, one of India's best milk breeds. There are Murrah buffaloes. There are displays of white rats that have been living on different diets. The poultry section would surpass an exhibit in a county fair in Iowa. Improved seeds, improved practices of farms and orchards and gardens—one huge mosaic on this 330-acre demonstration farm! This fair is a pageant vividly portraying the agricultural improvement Jack De Valois has brought to South India during the past thirty-four years.

Another day you may want to visit Katpadi to see the Eye Camp. Men patients with bandaged eyes are lying on the floor in one room of the dormitory. Across the hall, also on the floor, are women patients, bandaged like the men.

Fifty men and women have had cataracts removed from their eyes in this one day. Most of them will have their sight restored.

Dr. Bernadine De Valois, "Bernie" as her husband Jack calls her, is a highly-trained physician and surgeon. She teaches four days a week in the Vellore Christian Medical College. Mrs. John, the wife of the Katpadi Indian extension worker, is also a doctor. Clinics and dispensaries are a part of the institute's extension program.

By this time you realize that this mission station has four sides: religion, agriculture, health, and education. We will let Jack De Valois explain these four phases of work in his own words.

"We have a farm school with sixty-three boarding students and 201 pupils in the day school," Jack begins. "We have what Gandhi called basic education. It's similar to the vocational agriculture taught in American high schools. Our boys, to a large extent, raise their own vegetables, cereals, milk, and other necessities."

You can see for yourself as you and Mr. De Valois walk around the farm. He points out the various facilities as you go.

"These twenty acres we've set aside for a camp site

Below, winnowing rice at Katpadi. At bottom of page, Mr. DeValois proudly inspects one of the mission dairy cows.

and for conference purposes. Here's the chapel. This is the guest house. That's the dining hall. Several conferences and retreats are held here each year. You should have been here last week at our Workers' Conference. We had more than seven hundred registered delegates."

You ask more about the extension program.

"We have twelve model village poultry units and a cooperative that markets approximately 300,000 eggs a year for the members," he tells you. "We have three branch poultry farms that provide hatching eggs and improved strains of laying hens.

"On our 330-acre farm we produce all classes of livestock, also fruit, grain, and vegetables."

Before leaving Katpadi, you ask, "What is India's greatest need?"

"Some say it's religion; some say it's irrigation. Some say a public health program is our greatest need. Of course, more and better schools are needed. We here at Katpadi are trying to tackle all phases in one integrated program. With our moving pictures we reach some fifty thousand people a year. The films deal with religion, agriculture, and health.

"We had thirty thousand people enter the gates during our annual Rural Fair this year. It has outgrown our wildest expectations.

"We finished cleaning the fair grounds by 10 P.M. Saturday night and jumped right into a conference of the Student Christian Movement on Sunday morning at eight o'clock."

As you leave India and Mr. De Valois at his Katpadi station, you remember that he mentioned Gandhi and his basic education. Perhaps you will recall how this Indian prophet in homespun won India her independence by waging, not war, but peace.

Both peace and war demand great sacrifice, but peace will never really be won on the basis of self-interest. It can be won only by sharing with others. Jack and Dr. Bernadine De Valois demonstrate their belief in this principle by the dedicated work they are doing at Katpadi.

103

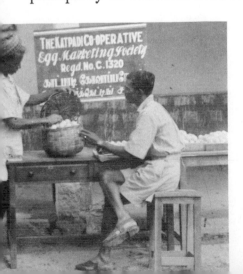

The Katpadi Cooperative helps farmers keep a steady and profitable market for their eggs.

a rural Christian center in Burma

M arian Hackett, Bill's wife, is "stuck." She's been translating the Gospels into Taungthu. That's the language used in the part of Burma where she and Bill are stationed. She checks it against the English translation, then the Greek. Then she tries it out on a group of Taungthu people to see if the meaning is clear. She's in the *Acts of the Apostles* now.

But she's stuck on a translation. It concerns the words "to serve" and "servant." The Taungthu language can say "slave" or "one who is hired," but there is no word for "serve" as used in the Gospels.

Besides her translation work, she manages her home with two children, conducts classes in sewing and literacy, and has fifty or sixty callers a week. A few more callers won't matter.

So you visit Bill and Marian Hackett, Baptist missionaries in Burma.

"Where's Bill?" you ask.

"He's away most of the time," Marian begins. "A man came after him yesterday from a village some ten miles from here. The man said the people of his village were sick and dying. This man had heard Bill preach at a Buddhist festival over there seven months ago.

"When the man came, he asked Bill if he really meant it when he said in his sermon over there that he wanted to help people who were in trouble. From what the man said we knew that the people there had cholera, probably complicated with bacillary dysentery.

"So Bill jumped on his motorbike and hurried to the hospital in Taunggyi for sulfa pills and some injections. Then he took Nurse Sayama Wirsay and went back with the man."

Mrs. Hackett glanced behind the house and continued, "I see he took the truck. He uses a motorbike, a jeep, or a truck, depending on the weather and the roads and whether medicine or pigs or delegates to a Youth Conference are to be transported."

Workworn Burmese farmers look forward to brighter futures for their sons. Below, Bill Hackett with the truck that helps him keep going his rounds.

"What is the history of this Rural Christian Center, Mrs. Hackett?"

"When Bill and I came to Burma as missionaries, we lived in a big brick house in the city of Taunggyi. Our mission has a church, a school, and a hospital there. But Burma's population is 80 per cent rural. Soon Bill discovered that young people who come to city institutions seldom, if ever, return to the village to live and to serve.

"In February, 1945, Bill got this eighteen-acre farm five miles out. The buildings went up in this order: tool shed, chicken house, pig house, cattle shed, dispensary, missionary's home, elementary school, and church."

"What did the people think of your farm, Mrs. Hackett?"

"Well," she answers, "we call it a Rural Christian Center. Always before, a church was a church, a school was a school, and a hospital was a hospital. The idea of having a missionary center on a dirt road, experimenting with new seeds, raising pigs and chickens, baptizing converts, running a dispensary and a school, all at one place and by the same missionary, certainly was novel to the people.

"They asked us some interesting questions when we first came."

105

"What kind of questions did they ask?" you want to know.

"They'd ask, 'Why do your Berkshire pigs grow twice the size of our long-snouted pigs in the same length of time and with the same feed?

" 'Why do your White Leghorn hens lay so many more eggs than our jungle many-colored flocks?' "

You ask about crops.

"Bill had some crops they had never seen before, Florida Yellow Dent corn, and Hickory King Hominy corn. Yes, and oats, alfalfa, cabbage, cauliflower, and tomatoes.

"Soon pigs, chickens, grain, and garden seeds began to sell like hot-cakes. Little pigs were promised before they were born. They've been flown by air to all parts of Burma.

"But I think the most curious sight was the hydraulic ram. Folks couldn't understand how water could flow uphill and provide running water for each house."

She goes on to tell how the people came first through curiosity, then as friends, and later as neighbors. Soon they began asking how they could help. More than seventy-five men came with their carts and hauled stone to build a dam for the water system. Many working bees were held when the buildings were going up. More than four hundred man-days of labor were contributed. It has become *their* center.

You learn that within two years the school program with one hundred pupils became 45 per cent self-supporting. Mrs. Hackett keeps the books. The medical program is 50 per cent self-supporting, the church and evangelistic program 60 per cent self-supporting, and the farm now is paying its way. Bill has a nurse, a farm manager, a pastor, and three teachers helping him.

106

"Here comes Bill's truck now!"

He seems young, tall, strong—able to do almost any kind of job. Burma-born, he is a graduate of Drury College with a Ph.D. from Cornell College of Agriculture.

"Sorry to keep you waiting," he begins. "I don't seem to have any schedule. Our Christmas was a week late last year."

Row planting of potatoes saves many hours over the former method, even when the work must be done by hand.

You have never heard before of a late Christmas, so you ask, "How did it happen?"

"Our nurse was called to a nearby village to a case that turned out to be the dreaded killer, pneumonic plague. The patient died within twenty-four hours. Soon another case was brought to the dispensary. I jumped on my motor bike and hurried away to the hospital for serum. News was sent to the adjoining villages about this dreaded disease, with word for all to come for injections. People came who never before had been to the center. More than twelve hundred people were inoculated, so many that our Christmas Festival had to be postponed a week.

"When the festival finally was held a week late, the people began coming about ten o'clock. By eleven the crowd numbered at least one thousand, and the preacher began explaining the meaning of Christmas.

"Then the crowd was asked to sit on the grass, and the local church members passed out their 'five loaves and two fishes' to thirteen hundred people.

"About one o'clock the congregation went down to the stream to witness the baptism of new converts, the first to come out of Buddhism from some of the villages. By three o'clock all gathered around a temporary stage for the Christmas pageant, given by one hundred children from our school at the center.

"We felt the Christ Child came, even though he was a week late.

"I can see the day when most of these people will be Christian. It's a dream worth working and praying for."

Simple methods of erosion control, such as that being demonstrated to these hill men, conserve much valuable soil.

down the river in Borneo

You hear people talk about going to the far ends of the earth. That's Borneo.

It's an island somewhat larger than Texas, in jungle land. The equator runs through the middle. The scenery and the heat are superlative. There are two seasons, the "dry" season when it rains hard every day, and the rainy season when the skies drip all the time, day and night, which adds up to an average of 157 inches of rainfall a year.

But the church is there. In Sarawak (Sah-rah′wahk), a colony on the north side of Borneo, there are nineteen American missionaries writing an amazing story, building a Christian civilization in place of jungle savagery.

You come down in the heart of Borneo, far up the Rejang River in the land of the Dyaks, formerly head-hunters, where you see strange long-house villages. Regardless of a few well-smoked skulls and some hunting knives hanging on the walls, the people are very friendly.

A whole village of some twenty-five families lives in one long narrow bamboo and wood house extending the length of a city block in your home town in America. Each family of perhaps six people has one big room leading out to the common veranda. The longhouse,

Mr. and Mrs. Harris teach by demonstrating: caring for livestock, digging in the garden, instructing Dyak children.

usually on a hillside, is up fifteen or twenty feet on stilts, giving an unsightly view of pigs or chickens underneath.

At Nanga Mujong, Tom and Jennie Harris are running an Agricultural Training Center. Mr. Harris, who studied agriculture at Florida A. and M. College, cleared this jungle, built a school and a church, and by his extension program is demonstrating a better way of life. But first he had to learn about the Dyaks and why they need help.

"They are animists," Mr. Harris explains, "which means that their way of life is based on fear. When their one crop of rice runs out, it is because of evil spirits. When a contagious disease spreads from family to family along the common veranda of the longhouse, it is also the curse of an evil spirit. When a baby dies because its mother knows of no suitable food for it, an evil spirit killed the child."

Tom and Jennie Harris are demonstrating with fertilizer and compost how to grow two crops of rice a year instead of one. Along with every sermon they preach goes a sample of

garden seeds. Poultry and pigs round out the farm school curriculum.

When Sunday rolls around, Mr. and Mrs. Harris are especially busy. Sunday school and church are followed by Bible study and literacy classes for adults. While the men's class and the women's society meet, Tom and Jennie are giving first aid to the sick.

Finally the crowd is off again for home and another week of routine activities, but now with a belief that life can be better than it is.

From here you go down the Rejang River in a long boat hollowed out of a log and powered by an outboard motor. Along the river's whispering shores are to be found eleven hundred varieties of ferns and eight hundred varieties of orchids.

The strange sounds of the tropics startle you as monkeys play or fight in the foliage to the accompaniment of strident and jangling notes of brilliantly-plumaged birds or the harsh call of gigantic insects. Nature has surpassed man in the green jungles of Sarawak.

Finally you arrive at Sibu to meet William Overholt, an Iowa-trained agriculturist, one of the nineteen Methodist missionaries in this jungle-covered island. He takes you up to his rambling one-story bungalow built on stilts eight or ten feet above the ground.

"The mission," he says, "owns a four-hundred-acre tract of land covered with rubber trees, the income from which has built churches and helps to support our thirty-three pastors."

Mr. Overholt's first big task is to improve the soil.

"Ours is probably the poorest soil in the tropics," he explains. "All the land is intensely acid. Only the coarsest grasses grow.

"I'm using forty acres of this farm for experiments with leguminous green manure crops for soil improvement and forage. I have thirty-five different kinds of tropical legumes.

"Also, I have started some kudzu, getting ready for my herd of milch goats. I obtained some improved seed corn from the Point Four men in Java.

"We're making new land, finding new crops, and helping to make new people."

There are sixty-one churches in the mission program. The smallest school has seventy-five pupils, but enrollment usually approaches two hundred.

Sarawak in Borneo is a long distance from America. The church is building a friendly road to that strange land under the equatorial sun where dwell more than a half-million of God's children.

why agricultural missionaries?

When Burl Slocum went to the Philippines in 1948 he found 180 Baptist churches in his five provinces. But 144 of them were without pastors, because they were unable to support a minister.

Mr. Slocum tells you that 90 per cent of the churches in his field are rural.

"The average Filipino farmer," he says, "cultivates only five acres and has a yearly income of only $250. Seven out of ten of the Filipino farmers are tenants. Because of inadequate credit facilities, if a tenant must borrow a bushel of rice from his landlord, he pays back two.

"Eighty per cent of the 21 million Filipinos are farmers and yet the daily per capita food supply is only 60 per cent of what the average American gets. The Filipino farmer is not able to support a church with a resident pastor.

"Population is increasing in the Philippines at the rate of a half-million a year, but the yield of rice, corn, chickens, hogs, cattle, and carabaos is decreasing. Because of erosion, the top soil is gone from 34 per cent of the land."

These facts present problems and more problems, as you can see.

When Mr. Slocum went to the Philippines as an agricultural missionary for the Baptist Church, he had three advantages. He was a graduate in agriculture from Wisconsin, with additional study at Cornell. He had had teaching experience. Also, he had been an extension specialist for six years at Washington State College of Agriculture and five years at Cornell.

"When I came," he begins, "I found a lot of political appointees who were supposed to carry on an agricultural extension program. Unfortunately, they had not had an opportunity to be trained for their work. Immediately, I started classes in extension methods for them at their own request.

Many small rural churches like this one have been unable to support pastors. Agricultural missions help them become self-supporting.

Mr. Slocum's greatest interests are the boys and girls and the humble homes around his mission.

"After four years, a national agricultural extension service was inaugurated here in the Philippines similar to the American county agent plan.

"Next came 4-H Clubs. In order to make any permanent improvement in farm life, it is necessary to start with the youth.

"Soon it became apparent that before much club work could be done, it would be necessary to prepare 4-H Club material.

112

"Within three years I prepared and published twenty-three different 4-H Club bulletins. The one on poultry diseases and parasites is in its third printing. These bulletins now are being used extensively throughout the islands.

"Each of the thousand boys and girls in our clubs in this section demonstrates better methods, and his or her project is a demonstration of improved agriculture in the *barrio*.

"Next came what we called Rural Institutes, for adults. They were not very successful, so we changed to what we called Farm Study Classes. They are three-year courses. There are 2,274 farmers enrolled. These farmers meet for three hours each week. The first is for a lecture; the other two hours are for demonstration.

"At the end of the three-year course, farmers are given the award of Successful Farmer.

"Four bulletins were prepared for these young farmers' clubs, more than nine hundred pages of material. Also, I prepared a 150-page *Teacher's Guide* and *Student Study Manual* for high schools.

"In 1950, our Baptist Central Philippine University, here at Iloilo, started a School of Agriculture. We started with 47 students; now we have 137. I have five teachers to help me. We are getting a new man from America next year, who comes from North Carolina with a Doctor's degree in agriculture.

"Since 1952, our thirty-acre college farm has been used for demonstration purposes. We produce improved seeds and livestock for the use of our 4-H Clubs and farm study courses."

"Mr. Slocum, you're a missionary sent out by the Baptist Church. How is all your work related to the Filipino church?"

"In the first place," he says, "we are trying to make the *barrio* or community financially able to support a church and a resident minister.

"In the second place, we are supplementing the training of our ministers. Now, our ministerial students have a five-year course, including arts and sciences the first and second years, agriculture the third year, and Bible and Christian doctrine the fourth and fifth years.

"We want the pastor to be able to lead his community not only in better agriculture, but in all phases of improved rural life. We want him to be partially self-supporting by the use of his garden and small animals."

Rice mills in the Philippines travel from farm to farm. At left, a Filipino rice thresher is at work. Mr. Slocum's demonstrations in proper plant spacing have greatly increased the yield.

Mr. Slocum shows the sun porch type of chicken house recommended for farmers with small flocks. He has prepared and published many bulletins on methods for 4-H Clubs.

As Mr. Slocum walks about the college farm with you and proudly shows you his Durocs and Berkshires, his White Leghorns and Hampshires, his Indian Runner ducks and his Bronze turkeys, his Toggenberg goats and his Vellore cattle, you discover that he is well trained for his job. You realize that he is changing the lives of the boys and the girls and the young farmers in their humble homes. In addition, he is improving the little churches in the *barrios* of his 4,448 square miles on Panay Island.

As you are about to leave you ask, "Why did you come to the Philippines, Mr. Slocum?"

"God made it clear to me," he says, "that he wished me to go as an agricultural missionary, because the need in the mission field is much greater abroad than in America."

A wayside home, shaded by foliage and boasting a fine papaya tree. The average farm in the Philippines is small, about five acres.

from torpedo boat to mission farm

When a suicide plane hit a motor torpedo boat in the Philippines, Raymond Hill, a farm youth from Indiana, was one of the eight rescued. While recovering from his wounds in a hospital there, he had two months to think about his future. Eight years to the day after he left the Philippines in uniform, he was back again to begin a new type of service.

On New Year's Day, 1952, he started operations on a 2,500-acre mission farm on the island of Mindanao (Min-dah-nah'oh). Already he has five hundred acres under cultivation. In June, 1953, he and his colleagues started their new Mountain View College, with an enrollment of two hundred students the first year.

As you visit this farm, you notice immediately its natural beauty. It is a broad, level plain surrounded by cool mountains and scenic waterfalls. The 2,500-foot elevation gives a cool and delightful climate in a land of year-round growing weather. You notice a forest of sixty-foot trees, three or four feet in diameter, and a sawmill busy at work.

"What are these trees, Mr. Hill, and what are you doing with them?"

"These are the finest of mahogany," he explains. "We expect to have fifteen hundred acres of our farm used as a commercial mahogany forest.

"Our students work on the farm with their teachers in the forenoon and attend classes in the afternoon. The sun usually shines here during the forenoons, but our afternoon showers add up to an average of 120 inches of rainfall a year.

"We sawed all the lumber for our school buildings out of these trees.

"But we raise other crops. We have five hundred acres under cultivation now. Soon we'll be farming one thousand acres. We raise bananas, papayas, pineapples, mangoes, and all kinds of citrus fruit.

"I guess you've heard of the famous Manila rope. We grow hemp that goes into that rope.

"We raise much of the food for our two hundred students. Rice, corn, poultry, and cattle are grown.

"We are fortunate in being in a section that has neither typhoons nor outlaws."

"What is the matter with the Philippines, Mr. Hill, that makes it necessary for a mission board to have a school like this?"

"All phases of agriculture here," he explains, "are still suffering from the war. The livestock is gone. There are almost no carabaos nor cattle for draft power. Of course that has affected crop production. The standard of living is very low. Eighty per cent of the 21 million Filipinos are farmers, but it's a peasant type of agriculture.

"Of our two hundred students, forty are majoring in agriculture.

"We give them the basic science courses. Then they study irrigation and drainage, plant propagation and nursery management, vegetable raising and the principles of crop production. We teach farm motors and machinery. We have room on this island for farm machinery. Every student includes Bible study in each semester and every student learns a supplementary trade."

"What about your future plans here, Mr. Hill?" you ask.

"You noticed that beautiful waterfall as you entered the winding road coming up here to the campus. That's 120 feet high. We are planning to use that to operate a hydroelectric plant. We plan to produce our own light and power. You see, we're far out in the interior of this island, miles from any city center.

Planting time brings out the tractor and drill. At far right, a bag of peanuts is the focal point around which Mr. Hill and some of his co-workers gather to register their satisfaction for the camera.

"Also, out here in this field," says Mr. Hill, pointing to one of the few level cleared fields, "we plan to build a landing strip. We hope to have a flag stop here at the school for the Philippine Air Lines."

"Mr. Hill, this seems an isolated place to build a school. If you'd located in Manila or some large city, wouldn't it have been easier?"

"Most of the Filipinos live in lonely and isolated *barrios* like this. As for myself, I feel at home here.

"I remember that when I was a little boy on a farm in Indiana my father built a small seat in front of his on a cultivator. I went with him to the field. He told me I was helping him plow the corn.

"My church, my 4-H Club, and my vocational agriculture classes trained me for this type of life. I remember that I used to enjoy a corn-husking contest as much as a basketball game.

"Then came the war. I saw the needs in New Guinea, South America, and in the Philippines. When I went home I studied agriculture six years, earning two degrees. Then for two years I taught agriculture.

"My church and mission, the Seventh-day Adventist, give liberally to support this type of work. We are a small church, but more than 90 per cent of our people are tithers.

"It's great to work where you are needed, when you are prepared, and when your church at home stands behind you."

This junior college is located at Malaybalay, on Mindanao.

You recall that a mutual defense treaty between the United States and the Philippines was ratified on March 20, 1952, agreeing "separately and jointly to resist attacks from the outside." The two governments proposed to help each other fight communism, which breeds on hunger and disease among landless peasants in the Far East.

Mr. Hill is fighting hunger, disease, and landless peasantry with scien-   **117**
tific agriculture and practical religion.

a hospital on wheels

Come along with Dorothy Edwards Crisologo, who travels as far as halfway around the world every year. She runs a mobile medical clinic in the Philippines.

If you never have seen a hospital on wheels, here it is.

The body of a truck is built with compartments for medical equipment and supplies. Wooden crates can be taken out as needed. The jeep and trailer take over in the mountains. Along with this health mobile goes Mrs. Crisologo, herself a trained nurse working under the Methodist Woman's Division of Christian Service, and her Filipino staff: Dr. Crisologo, the physician she recently married; Dr. Sison, dentist; Freddie Tabije, mechanic; and Miss Cabanilla, nurse.

"Why not stay in one place, Mrs. Crisologo? Why so much traveling?"

"Here in the Philippines," she explains, "we have only half as many doctors per one thousand population as countries like Mexico, Cuba, or Chile, and most of our doctors are in the city centers. We have only one doctor to every four thousand people. That's roughly one fifth what you have in America. Our Mobile Medical Clinic serves the rural people in the more isolated sections. We conduct our clinic a week at each place, usually in cooperation with the pastor of the local church.

"We treat an average of sixty patients per day, but we sometimes have as many as 150 in one day. Also, we conduct classes in first aid, home nursing, nutrition, prenatal and infant care. Personal and individual instruction is given to each patient. Sometimes this calls for a home visit.

"For example, one evening I was making a visit to the home of a patient with tuberculosis, giving instruction to the sister on follow-up care of the patient. As I came down the ladder out of the little bamboo hut, a middle-aged woman approached me, pleading that I come immediately to see her sick friend.

118

Mrs. Crisologo prepares to board a plane with medical supplies, for a hop-off to Mindanao Island.

" 'She's dying!' the woman cried.

"I hurried back to the clinic, called the doctor, and filled our emergency bag. We drove eight miles down the highway, left the jeep at the crossroads, and started to hike. Darkness was overtaking us fast. Soon it was pouring rain. The trail became slippery. We were drenched. The lightning helped us see our direction. I took an occasional tumble over a stone or slippery slope. After two hours, we began to pass a few thatched-roof bamboo houses, and our guide led us into a room dimly lighted with a flickering kerosene torch. A small group of people hovered over a prostrated body that was lying limply on the floor in one corner.

"At first I thought the patient was dead. She was in a critical condition. The diagnosis was made—malaria.

"After emergency treatment, we instructed the family to carry her by hammock to the road the following day. We met them there and transported her by jeep and stretcher to our clinic.

"In a week she was walking. Her family in another island had been notified by wire of her critical condition. Their return telegram said, 'Please embalm her. We are coming!'

"You can imagine their joy when she met them walking."

119

The mobile clinic where as many as one hundred patients are treated in a single day.

Mrs. Crisologo explains that this was not a typical evening.

"We carry on our medical work during the day, and usually in the evening we hold evangelistic services.

"I think eighty decisions for Christ was the highest number we have had any one evening.

"Visitation evangelism is the method we find best. One staff member and one local church member join together, and we go out two by two, visiting the prospective members in the community where we are holding the clinic. In one place, in a period of only two days there were twenty-five decisions. In many places, this visitation continues long after the clinic leaves."

You learn that this hospital on wheels covered five thousand miles in one year and served 8,628 patients in sixty different communities. Mrs. Crisologo's jeep traveled 14,500 miles in one year, as far as halfway around the world.

Sometimes the country is so rough that the truck and trailer can't make it, but the doctors and nurses must get through. For example, after holding a clinic in the *barrio* of Nemmatan, the team went to Napolong.

Since the truck couldn't make those roads, Mrs. Crisologo and her team used a caravan of eleven carabao sleds on which the equipment was dragged. When they came to a river, they placed the sleds on a bamboo raft, and the carabaos swam ahead furnishing the "power."

At left, Miss Cabanilla uses a chart to teach prenatal care to young mothers-to-be. At right, visual instruction in child care is given at the mobile clinic.

"It was here," Mrs. Crisologo explains, "that we witnessed the dramatic recovery of a baby who would surely have died had she not received medical treatment.

"The pastor had traveled over his circuit, informing all the surrounding *barrios* of the coming of the clinic. There was one young mother who heard the news and, as a last resort, wrapped her dying baby in a blanket and walked three miles to the clinic. This four-month-old baby had been weak from birth. A few days before our arrival the baby had developed dysentery, complicated with bronchopneumonia. She was grayish-blue and so listless that she did not whimper, even when given several injections. The mother, undernourished, was in rags and penniless. She had lost two other children because of a similar malady, and her heart was breaking when the doctor explained to her the seriousness of this child's condition. Provision was made for this mother and baby to stay in the house with the doctor and nurses for several days.

"All night we took turns getting up every three hours to administer the necessary medicines or feedings of glucose that had to be given by injection. All night that little life hung by a thread, and all night that anxious mother watched over her baby, looking to us for words of reassurance.

"The next day the child showed marked improvement, and before we left this place she had recovered completely. In the days the mother was with us she learned how to care for her baby and began to understand it was not evil spirits that caused her child's dysentery, but bacteria from the river water she was drinking.

"At the close of the Sunday morning service, our last day in this *barrio*, the young mother came to the altar with her restored baby in her arms. There she knelt on the hard cement floor and, with tears of joy streaming down her face, gave thanks to her new-found Christ for saving her baby and herself."

121

As you leave Mrs. Crisologo and her mobile clinic, you learn that such experiences do not happen just once or twice a year, but similar instances occur day after day.

These islands of 21 million people need more ambassadors of good will like Dorothy Edwards Crisologo, from Genoa, New York.

the poor man's bank

Visited 51 churches
Attended 339 meetings
Preached 22 sermons
Wrote bulletins and articles and one book
Helped organize credit unions

This is a part of an annual report of Allen Huber, a missionary of the Disciples Church in the Philippines.

"Mr. Huber, in your report you say you organize credit unions. This seems a bit unusual. Why do you, a busy missionary with so much other work, spend time organizing credit unions?"

"Here in the Philippines capital is scarce," Mr. Huber explains. "Interest rates are extremely high. Poverty is everywhere. Credit unions solve these problems of credit for the masses. They are the poor man's bank."

"Why does the poor man need a bank?"

"It teaches him to save something from whatever he earns. It provides capital for productive purposes at a reasonable rate of interest. It trains him in the wise use of his money.

"Back in 1938, we organized our first credit union. It took ten meetings. Since then 126 such cooperatives have been set up. They've loaned more than a million and a quarter pesos ($625,000). Some day we hope to have twenty thousand credit unions in the islands, one for every one thousand of the population. We think they will help in the economic emancipation of the people."

"It is a little difficult to think in such large numbers. It would be easier to learn about one credit union at a time."

"Here's the Batac Credit Union, which grew within two years to 590 members. It has helped 610 borrowers. That means children have been

A pastor recommends a student for a loan to complete his education. The treasurer considers his appraisal, for character is the usual collateral in credit union loans.

educated. Homes have been built. Rice lands have been purchased. Medical assistance has been obtained. Deceased loved ones have been buried.

"In all this, the members have relied upon their own resources, not on government aid.

"Here's another credit union that has helped forty-five families build their own homes.

"Our churches have a church-erection credit union. We have helped fifteen congregations construct new buildings. This money has come largely from their own savings.

"One of our unique organizations is composed entirely of ministers. We plan to have two thousand members and 100,000 pesos in share capital. Ministers usually call one another brother. We're trying to practice brotherhood. But it's a self-help program. In a practical way, it works out to the remotest minister in the most isolated village on the islands.

"Most of our credit unions are local. Democracy, you know, is a grassroots proposition. It is out in the country, where the need is greatest to remove the shackles of usury. What hope is there for a farmer who borrows five pesos in August and must pay his debt with a sack of rice worth fifteen pesos when harvest comes? This means debt for his family, for his children, for his children's children! It is among these landless debt-ridden farmers that communism thrives.

"If the church in the Philippines would champion the needs of the landless, debt-ridden, despairing farmers, we would not have room in our chapels for the crowds of worshipers. Many are Communists because no other group has taken an interest in their desperate plight.

123

"As you travel around in our islands, you will see the work of our 126 credit unions. You will see the hundreds of new homes being erected. You will see the rice lands, livestock, plows, and seed being purchased. You will learn of the hundreds of children being educated and many parents freed from debt and bondage. This will show you how people can be enabled to help themselves."

This missionary, Allen Huber, has endeared himself to the Filipino people. They speak affectionately of his unselfish efforts to help them organize their lives for self-help and Christian service.

The bell and tower of the church at Makati, Rizal, were made possible through the Church Erection Credit Union.

Members of the Pasay City Christian Church ride to service in "jeepneys" that credit union loans helped to buy. Homes like the one being "tidied" at the right have also benefited from loans.

home-grown democracy

Silverio Rodriguez is in a bad humor. He has just told his daughter, Prudencia, she must break a date. Why? She didn't consult her father first. What irked him most was that she said their pastor believes in what he calls democracy in the home.

Just then the pastor comes to the door. He asks Rodriguez to join him and two other men of the church in building two sanitary toilets on the church grounds.

When Rodriguez returns he starts giving his wife a lecture about, of all things, the various phases of Christian family life. The pastor must have done something to him. He informs his wife he is going to build a sanitary toilet, similar to the ones at the church, for their family on the back of their lot.

"Things are changing here in the Philippines," he informs her, with increasing emphasis. "The old days of squatting back of the bushes or trees in the back yard are over."

Supper is ready now, and the family begins the meal with the father saying his usual grace. The family doesn't completely approve of the meal Mrs. Rodriguez has prepared. They don't like her green and yellow vegetables. They don't care to eat papaya and calamansi "simply to get vitamins." They "never did like buffalo milk," and she should know that by this time.

"Give me rice, pork, and sweet potatoes after this," says Mr. Rodriguez, which should settle the question forever, since he is the head of the house. After supper he goes to the cockpit, as usual, to spend the evening with the other men.

Prudencia goes to a distant well to carry the family supply of water. "Children are to be seen and not heard!" How many times has she heard that! When will she be a young lady?

New possibilities in family life are being realized in the Philippines through the dedicated work of Ortha Lane. At right, a typical rural home; one of the small, alert boys who add joy to the work; a young married couple who hope for a secure future.

After Mrs. Rodriguez gets all the babies in bed, she sits down with a long sigh and wonders, "Do all families complain and quarrel as much as mine?" Her two-room house, with more children than furniture, is her entire world.

But things are really beginning to change in the Philippines, for people like the Rodriguez family. Ortha Lane, a highly-trained specialist in family life, is there. She was sent by the Woman's Division of Christian Service of the Methodist Church. She is an Iowa farm girl with her Ph. D. from the State University of Iowa. Her training and experience reach to several countries. She is in charge of the Department of Home and Family Life of the Federation of Churches in the Philippines.

One week in each December in the Philippines is designated as National Family Week by proclamation of the president. Miss Lane's committee, with other civic groups, makes out a daily program for all the islands. For the past three years, the themes have been Strong Families Make a Strong Nation, Cooperating Families Make Cooperating Communities, and A Strong Family Is Closely United and Well Informed.

On Family Sunday, couples stand together in church and renew their marriage vows. Families sit together in pews labeled with the family name on white cards entwined with beautiful pink cadena de amor.

Books and bulletins on family life are being written. Miss Lane's department operates a loan library with 340 different books on what family life should be. These are being sent all over the islands.

There is no divorce in the Philippines. The law doesn't allow it. Legal

separation may be granted under certain conditions, but there can be no remarriage for either party. Preparation for marriage is a large part of the program of the Christian Family Life Movement. Interfaith marriages are opposed. Marital counseling is a part of the program of the church

Miss Lane and her committee conduct area Family Life Conferences, and there was one such conference in 1954 that covered all of East Asia.

Mr. and Mrs. Silverio Rodriguez and many others are being reached at these conferences. Look at some of the subjects that are discussed: Living Together in the Family, Teaching Our Children Religion in the Home, Marital Counseling, Health of the Family, Economic Family Problems, and Democracy in the Home.

127

The Department of Home and Family Life seeks to reach every family in the Philippines by a fifteen-minute radio program each evening at 7:45.

This is the work of a girl who lived on a farm four miles from Solon, Iowa, and who attended a country school there. When she was graduated from West Liberty High School, a neighbor woman gave her a book as a commencement present. It was a story about a missionary, and it was called *Under Marching Orders*. As a result of that book, Miss Lane has been marching ever since in the underdeveloped countries of the world.

She is helping to bring Christian democracy to the homes of 21 million Filipinos.

from city schools to country homes

Miss Thomasine Allen, of Japan, has built a new road for young women to travel. She has developed a new missionary pattern for unmarried missionaries. She moved from institutions bounded by four walls out to where the people live.

"What changed your whole pattern of missionary work, Miss Allen?" you ask her.

"Back in 1933 we had a famine here in Japan, followed by a tidal wave," she explains. "That sent me out of my teaching job in our mission school at Sendai to do relief work in Iwate Prefecture far to the North.

"When I saw the needs of these rural people, I didn't wait for any more arguments. One of these counties, called Ku No He, had 100,000 people living on farms and in twenty towns and villages. I chose that county for my parish."

"What happened, Miss Allen?"

"First a kindergarten. Nobody works harder than these Japanese women. They're often in the field from six in the morning until eight at night. Mrs. Yahaba, our pastor's wife, and two other teachers now have 120 children in this day nursery.

"Next was a clinic. The infant mortality rate in our county averaged 50 per cent, but ran as high as 65 per cent in some villages. In six years that clinic has grown into a twenty-bed hospital and averages fifty out-patients per day. We have three Japanese doctors and four nurses."

"How is that different from any hospital in any little town in America?"

"Statistics don't tell much about the needs, do they? These are things that happen every day or two:

"A man living some fifteen miles out put his wife into a push cart, then transferred her to a bus, then to a push cart again, until he got her there. The doctor was able to save her life, but could not save her baby.

128

The consummation of a dream! The first of ten buildings constructed at the Christian Rural Center in Kuji.

"Finally some American churches sent me a station wagon with a four-wheel drive for these mountain roads. In just one night that station wagon brought to the clinic a man bitten by a poisonous snake, a boy with a bad case of pneumonia, and a woman who gave birth to twin girls. Five lives were saved that night.

"Next was our primary school. It started in 1951. I believe it was the first Christian primary school north of Tokyo."

"A woman can manage schools and health clinics, but can you do anything to improve agriculture, Miss Allen?"

"We have a Farmers' Gospel School each year, using government teachers. Besides, our pigs, chickens, rabbits, and potatoes from the center are sent out to the farms in considerable numbers."

"How about religion, evangelism, the church, and those things to which missionaries formerly gave all their time?"

"When we started here, there were only 237 farm villages with churches in all of Japan. In other words, only one village in forty had a church.

"In September, 1948, we had our first baptismal service. Fifteen young men and women told the story of their faith and were baptized. On Christmas Day of that year, we organized a church with fourteen more baptisms. Within two years, our Sunday school enrollment had reached two hundred. Now we have three branch stations.

"I believe the church is growing faster with this type of program."

"Miss Allen, do you feel you're on the right track, an unmarried woman running a Christian center away out here in the country?"

"Fifty and more years ago," Miss Allen says, "our mission boards established much-needed schools and hospitals in the cities. Most unmarried women then were sent to such institutions as teachers or nurses. Now, in many countries such as Japan, the government has many splendid schools and hospitals in the cities. But in every land, rural people are largely unserved or neglected. We have nearly nine thousand rural villages here in Japan still unchurched.

"Our Christian Rural Center has a staff of thirty workers and ten buildings. We reach a big rural area, which includes 100,000 people.

"It was discouraging here at first, but if you wish to see the rainbow you must wait until the storm is over."

You have seen the work of Miss Thomasine Allen (Tommie to her friends). She's a Baptist from Franklin, Indiana, who left her institution in the city of Sendai to establish a great rural Christian center in Kuji, Japan, the influence of which is touching the lives of the people in twenty towns and villages of her mountainous county.

"There is not enough darkness in all the world," Miss Allen says, "to put out the light of one small candle."

Miss Allen plays the piano for her kindergarten, and the children enjoy a good morning skip.

Japanese farm women are often literally up to their
knees in work. Women also work with their husbands
at the hard job of irrigating their small rice fields.

This is the main street in Kuji, which is
headquarters for Miss Allen's work.

a rural prophet in Japan

H ow and where should rural pastors be trained?" This question is apt to be discussed every time two or more missionaries get together. Edward Clark of Japan has one answer.

For eighteen years in Osaka and Kobe, he prepared students for the rural ministry, most of whom went to city churches as soon as they were graduated. This had been the pattern in Japan for ninety years. The rural churches were not able to support trained ministers. Churches had been established in 98 per cent of the cities in Japan and in 30 per cent of the towns, but in only one per cent of the rural townships. These 8,854 rural townships or farm villages without a church challenged this Presbyterian missionary from rural Minnesota, and he did something about it.

He selected one of his students, Mr. Junji Horii, to try a new plan for building a self-supporting rural parish. He asked his mission board to advance Mr. Horii's salary for the next ten years. With this money he bought a farm, planted fruit trees, added small animals, and built a modest farmhouse with one room in it suitable for a chapel. The pastor operated the farm while he carried on religious and social activities.

There were no members, no church building, no friends, nothing but suspicion, poverty, and appalling needs. Mr. Horii conducted farmers' institutes, lecture courses on agricultural improvements, and Peasant Gospel Schools. A weekly health clinic was held, and Mrs. Horii conducted a day nursery.

One day, some young farmers offered to help the pastor with his farm work, in appreciation of his service. They have been coming ever since.

The church farm soon seemed to some of the members too small for the expanding work, so they decided to dedicate to the church a little spot on their own farms. Even the poorest people gladly cultivated their Lord's *Tsubo* on each little two-acre farm.

Students pray before beginning the day's work. Appropriately, their morning chapel is a field under the open sky.

After seven years, seventy-nine people asked to be organized into a Christian church. This work is going forward steadily. At the present time the young laymen form teams and go out regularly to twenty neighboring hamlets to preach the message of this Imorino rural church.

After World War II, Mr. Clark returned to Japan to find it wide open for rural evangelism. The new government had bought 80 per cent of the fields formerly cultivated by tenants, nearly five million acres, and sold them to tenants on a twenty-four-year basis. Out of 2,600,000 tenants, 2 million were buying the land they cultivated. Tenancy was reduced from 50 per cent to 13 per cent. This was democracy's answer to communism. Soon a new agricultural law was passed, making possible farm cooperatives. Church attendance increased. A Sunday school could be started in practically any place, but almost no ministers were trained for rural work.

133

Mr. Clark and the Rural Committee of the interdenominational Church of Christ in Japan purchased a twenty-six-acre farm twenty-five miles west of Tokyo, near a small country town called Hino, and established a school there to train rural pastors and laymen for the type of work that Mr. Horii did at Imorino.

Seminary students spend the forenoon in the classroom and the afternoon on the farm. They earn while they learn. The land is double cropped with rice, wheat, corn, rye, barley, and many vegetables.

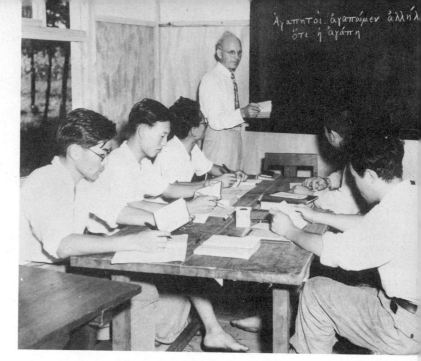

Dr. Clark teaches Greek to a class of beginning students at the training center.

There are nine hundred persimmon trees, in addition to walnut, pecan, and peach trees. Milk from the dairy, eggs from the poultry, and honey from the apiary are sold as well as used on the school table.

The average student earns his room and his food, and he learns how to become a partially self-supporting rural pastor.

Nearly every prefecture, from Hokkaido in the north to Kyushu in the south, is represented in the student body of this National Christian Rural Service and Training Center. Most of the students come from rural homes. This rural theological seminary has tended to keep its students rural in their interests and temperament instead of urbanizing them, as

134

The weighing of wheat is a task these students take seriously. The preparation of compost, seen at the bottom of the page, also requires workman-like concentration.

training in a city would have done. Agricultural Missions, Inc., which represents forty-five mission boards, recommends this type of training for the other fifty countries in which Protestant missionaries are at work.

Eighty-five per cent of those who have been graduated from this four-year course are engaged in Christian work in rural villages.

This seminary has an extension program and supervised field work.

With six million farm families freed from the burdens of a semifeudal land system after World War II, there is now in Japan a back-to-the-land movement. State Shinto is gone. The Emperor is divine no longer. Church and state are now separate. The doors are wide open for Christianity.

135

At far left, Mrs. Murono, wife of the director, prepares a meal in the temporary kitchen at the center. Near left, two girl students study while a small friend on the ledge amuses himself.

Abbreviations: BOT.—bottom; CEN.—center; EXC.—except; LT.—left; RT.—right; T.—top.

Cover: UNATIONS

iii: Press Information Bureau, Government of India

5: R. S. Beese from Photographic Service, Pennsylvania State College

6: Florine Cantrell

9: Black Star

10: Chim from Black Star

11: Black Star

12-15: United Christian Missionary Society

17: Hazel V. Orton

18: T.LT.—United Andean Mission; CEN.—W. Stanley Rycroft; BOT.—Hazel V. Orton

19: Hazel V. Orton

21: Canadian Baptist Foreign Mission Board; EXC.BOT.—Reliance Engravers, Ltd.

24: Hazel V. Orton from Methodist Prints

25: T.—E. E. Reed; CEN.—H. R. Ferger; BOT.—Hazel V. Orton (all from Methodist Prints)

26: E. E. Reed from Methodist Prints

28, 29: Alice Strangway

30: Committee on Missionary Education, United Church of Canada

34: ALL—Board of Foreign Missions, Presbyterian Church, U.S.A.

37: LT.—Goldberg from Photo Science Service, Cornell University; RT.—Fujihira from Monkmeyer

38: Boury from Three Lions

39: Griff Davis from Black Star

42, 43: ALL—Hal Thwing

46: Kenneth Enright

47: T.—Belgian Government Information Center; BOT.—Kenneth Enright

48-51: ALL—W. W. Reid from Methodist Prints

55: Agricultural Missions, Inc.

58-60: ALL—Robert Turnbull

62: ALL—Board of Foreign Missions, Presbyterian Church, U.S.A.

63: T.LT.—Board of Foreign Missions, Presbyterian Church, U.S.A.; T.RT.—S. Neale Alter; BOT.—Agricultural Missions, Inc.

66: Zaidis, Lahore, Pakistan

67: T.LT.—Zaidis, Lahore, Pakistan; T.RT. and CEN.—Laura MacLachlan; BOT.—Kisco Photo Service

69-71: ALL—F. E. Peter

74, 75: ALL—Gifford Towle

78, 79: ALL—Foreign Mission Commission, Church of the Brethren

80, 81: Ray Pippitt from Alan Shilin

82: Press Information Bureau, Government of India

84: Arthur Slater; EXC. CEN.—T. Moore

85: ALL—Arthur Slater

87-89: ALL—Board of Missions, Assemblies of God

90: H. G. Conger from Methodist Prints

91, 92: ALL—Asvin Studio, Secunderabad

93: John Patterson

95-97: ALL—W. W. Reid from Methodist Prints

98-100: ALL—Charlotte Wyckoff

102: T.LT.—Eugene Ten Brink; BOT. (2)—Ralph G. Korteling (all from Board of Foreign Missions, Reformed Church in America)

105: LT.—Ross Madden from Black Star; RT.—American Baptist Foreign Mission Society

107: Ross Madden from Black Star

108, 109: ALL—Woman's Division of Christian Service, Methodist Church

112: LT.—Methodist Prints; RT.—American Baptist Foreign Mission Society

113: LT.—J. Howard; RT.—J. W. Decker from American Baptist Foreign Mission Society

114: T.—J. W. Decker from American Baptist Foreign Mission Society; BOT.—Methodist Prints

115, 117: ALL—Raymond Hill

119: T.—C. L. Spottswood from Methodist Prints; BOT.—Methodist Prints

120: ALL—Methodist Prints

123, 124: ALL—Religious News Service

126: Armstrong Roberts

127: Todd Webb from Black Star

129: Thomasine Allen

130: Woman's American Baptist Foreign Mission Society

131: T.LT.—Herbert Lanks from Black Star; T.RT.—H. Armstrong Roberts; BOT.—Maurice Hodge Studio

133, 134: ALL—Board of Foreign Missions, Presbyterian Church, U.S.A.

135: T.—Board of Foreign Missions, Presbyterian Church, U.S.A.; BOT.—Agricultural Missions, Inc.

TYPE: TIMES ROMAN · COMPOSITION: RUTTLE, SHAW & WETHERILL, PHILADELPHIA · OFFSET LITHOGRAPHY: LATHAM PROCESS CORPORATION, NEW YORK · BINDING: CLOTH, CHAS. H. BOHN & CO., INC., NEW YORK; PAPER, LATHAM PROCESS CORPORATION, NEW YORK · TEXT PAPER: BECKETT BRILLIANT OPAQUE VELLUM · LAYOUT AND TYPOGRAPHICAL DESIGN: MARGERY W. SMITH · BINDING: LOUISE E. JEFFERSON · JACKET AND COVER DESIGN: WARREN JOHNSON.